Winding the Clock on the Independence Square

Jackson County's Historic Truman Courthouse

80th Anniversary Commemorative Edition

By David W. Jackson

Jackson County Historical Society
Independence, Missouri
December 2013

Jackson, David W. (1969-)
    Winding the Clock on the Independence Square: Jackson County's Historic Truman Courthouse
        244 p.   cm.
        Illustrations. Index.

ISBN-13: 978-069202136-1 (Jackson County Historical Society)
ISBN: 0692021361

First Edition, December 2013.

1. Courthouses--Missouri--Jackson County--History. 2. Public buildings--Missouri. 3. Architecture--American Influences. 4. Buildings--Independence Square (Independence, Mo.)--Guidebooks.
I. Jackson, David W. (1969-). II. Title.

With gratitude to J. Bradley Pace, Gloria Smith, and the Jackson County Historical Society Publishing Committee, for their invaluable service.

Published by:
Jackson County Historical Society
P.O. Box 4241
Independence, MO 64051
jchs.org

"I may be one of the few here outside of President Truman who can remember coming up here and sitting on this corner and watching the town wind the clock. And now we're rewinding the clock. This is…a focal point for Jackson County. The Square [is coming] back alive…"
Independence Mayor Don Reimal

Table of Contents

Introduction

Independence Square in Independence, Jackson County, Missouri, has been in the middle of some of the most pivotal events in local and U.S. history.

In 1821—just after Missouri statehood and five years before Jackson County was formed—freighters began transporting goods from Missouri to Santa Fe, then part of Mexico, and returning with Mexican goods and silver.

Early Mormon 'saints' ventured West in pursuit of religious freedom in the 1830s. Its Community of Christ denomination eventually selected Independence as its 'international headquarters.'

Then, in the early 1840s, emigrants traveling the Oregon Trail circled Independence Square. '49ers seeking gold in the California Territory embarked on the California Trail from Independence Square in 1849. Through the 1850s, thousands of travelers outfitted here for their six-month overland journey to the gold fields on the Pacific coast.

When Kansas was admitted as a Territory in 1854, tensions began to rise between settlers at the edge of the political boundary of the United States. The ensuing Border War and later Civil War lasting until mid-1865 left a devastating impact on the community and cultural landscape.

Harry S. Truman's start in elected politics in the 1920s eventually put Independence at center stage once again after he ascended to become the 33rd President of the United States. During his tenure as Judge of the County Court, then Presiding Judge of Jackson County, and later as Senator, Vice President, and President, Truman and others saw Independence through the Great Depression and the Second World War.

The Square continued to evolve through the middle of the 20th century. As this book's walking tour (Appendix B) illustrates, most of the buildings around the Square date from the late 1880s through the 1970s. Urban Renewal in the 1960s left its mark on the architecture of the Square until a revitalization based in historic preservation began in earnest in the mid-1990s . . . and continues today (2013).

Independence Courthouse Square, looking east on West Lexington Avenue, ca. 1940s.

Throughout this entire 185+year history, Jackson County's Courthouse on Independence Square has stood as a monument to the past and symbol for our future. As you will see, the courthouse building on the Square that pioneers rode around in wagons and buggies in the early 19th century survives to this day because of the foresight of our forbearers.

More than one third of Missouri's 114 counties boast courthouses over 100 years old. At the time of their construction many represented the most architecturally significant building in their county. These buildings were constructed at the "county seat," a town or city selected as the administrative center of its county. Often these county seat courthouses feature imposing and elaborate structural ornamentation, domes or clock towers alluding to the prosperity and pride of their citizenry.

Jackson County has the rare distinction of claiming two surviving 19th century courthouses:

1) the 1827 Log Jackson County Courthouse; and,

2) the first, permanent, brick, 1838 Jackson County Courthouse

J. Bradley Pace, past-president of the Jackson County Historical Society, and author of, "Survivors: A Catalog of Missouri's Remaining 19th Century County Courthouses," said, *There can be no doubt that they are today among the county's most tangible links with its past.*

The 1838 nucleus of the present courthouse structure on Independence Square turned 175-years-old in 2013. This notable anniversary coincided with the building's re-dedication after a complete restoration and adaptive reuse for the benefit of future generations of Jackson County citizens . . . and the many tourists who visit Independence each year.

SURVIVORS

A Catalog of Missouri's
Remaining 19th Century County Courthouses

J. BRADLEY PACE

After considerable planning, construction and expense, the courthouse you see today—which was last remodeled in 1933, during Harry S. Truman's tenure as Jackson County Presiding Judge—was re-dedicated in 2013 as Jackson County's Historic Truman Courthouse, recognizing the 80th Anniversary of Truman's Great Depression-era accomplishment.

"No other city in America conveys the entire broad span of a person's life who became President as does Independence, Missouri. Residents of, and visitors to Independence, not only have the unique opportunity to visit the Harry S. Truman National Historic Site and the Truman Library [and Museum], they have the opportunity to live in and

9

visit a Presidential community," according to Jon E. Taylor, historian for the Harry S. Truman National Historic Site. He continued, *"The Independence Courthouse and Square were places etched in the memory of Harry S. Truman.... Taken as a whole, they portray the life experience of one of our nation's most important 20ᵗʰ century presidents."*[1]

The recent restoration of the courthouse and surrounding square was much needed. Extensive interior and exterior projects included restoring long-lost parking to accommodate patrons at restaurants, a movie theater, a unique assortment of boutique shops, and the courthouse itself. We're ready for the next 80 years.

On Friday and Saturday nights from the 1930s to the 1960s, teenagers were seen cruising one way around the courthouse square in what was known as "winding the clock."

What a perfect 'time' to "wind the clock" as we look back on the history of Independence Square and Jackson County's Historic Truman Courthouse.

David W. Jackson
Independence, Missouri
December 2013

1827 Log Courthouse[2]

     Jackson County was established on December 15, 1826. In accordance with state law, commissioners (David Ward and Julius Emmons of Lafayette County, and John Bartleson of Clay County) were appointed to select the "county seat."[3] The first meeting of the Jackson County Court (analogous to today's Jackson County Legislature) occurred in the private home of John Young on May 21, 1827, in Independence. At this meeting, the Court directed that bids be sought for the building of a "temporary log courthouse, made of hewn logs."

     Soon thereafter construction bids were solicited. The Court appropriated $175, but accepted the low bid of $150 from Daniel P. Lewis, a relative of Daniel Boone.[4]

     Samuel Weston, a cabinetmaker, supplied the doors and windows.[5] The logs were hewn using a broadaxe wielded by Samuel Shepard, who had been 'hired out' as a slave by his owner, James Shepherd (note the variation in spelling). A biography of Shepard is provided in the following endnote.[6]

     Construction of the two-room log house, 36-feet long and 18-feet-wide, featuring a rock chimney in each room, and a puncheon floor (logs with one side hewn smooth) was completed by February 1828, in time for Andrew Jackson's presidential election, when it served as a polling place for Blue Township residents.

     It is said that at the time of its construction it was the last county courthouse between Independence and the Pacific Ocean. At this time the area that later became Independence Square was only a small clearing in the woods and, "the courthouse square was full of stumps...."[7]

     This log courthouse served county government as a courthouse only briefly. The County Court sold Lot 59 (where the 1827 Log Courthouse was located from 1827-1916), including the structure, to Smallwood V. Noland on February 6, 1832.[8]

Still, this temporary structure had many owners and uses through the years, including that of a private home. The logs remained in fairly good condition since the building had been weather boarded (i.e., sided) for most of the intervening years.

In 1916, the structure was donated to the City of Independence by Christian Ott, Jr., the Mayor of Independence. The building was originally located one block east of the Square at the corner of Lexington Avenue and Lynn Street, but later moved in 1916 to the old City Hall property one block south of the Square (107 West Kansas), where it has remained.[9]

1827 Log Jackson County Courthouse clad in siding at its original location on Lynn Street

For 55 years between 1917 and June 15, 1972, the 1827 log Courthouse was the headquarters of the Community Welfare League (today Community Services League), which provided County residents with emergency relief. Bess Truman was the League's second president, when she was Miss Bess Wallace.[10]

In 1932, a one room cabin of the same log construction style was added to the south side of the Log Courthouse. This ca. 1845 cabin had once been a private school under the tutelage of Miss Priscilla Armstrong (later Mrs. Aiken). After the Civil War, the cabin had been moved to serve

12

as the kitchen at the rear of the Wiley Aiken home, formerly in the 400 block of West Lexington Avenue (Spring and Lexington).[11]

At some point, an historic artifact may have been buried in the front lawn of the 1827 Log Courthouse…a slave auction block. However, no historical documentation has been found to substantiate this other than an informal recollection on file in the Jackson County Historical Society's Archives.[12]

When the 1933 Courthouse (derived from the 1838 courthouse) was under construction, Harry Truman and his colleagues on the Jackson County Court used this historic structure for their temporary meeting space to conduct county business. In 1970, voters of Jackson County replaced the governing three-member administrative "Court" with a new

**1827 Log Jackson County Courthouse
relocated in 1916 to 107 West Kansas Avenue**

Constitutional Home Rule Charter establishing a County Executive and the County Legislature. It was appropriate that the Log Courthouse hosted the very last meeting of the County Court on November 27, 1972. In 1981, the building underwent an additional restoration funded by the Independence Young Matrons and the City of Independence.

It is remarkable that this structure has survived for more than 175 years and remains open to the public. For a more complete history of the 1827 Log Jackson County Courthouse, consider visiting the site and taking a guided tour.

Santa Fe Trail
through Independence Square

       Before the town of Independence was platted, oxen-pulled Conestoga covered wagons passed through the area that became Independence Square on their way to-and-from Santa Fe in Mexico. Beginning in 1821, Santa Fe Trail traders from Franklin and Arrow Rock, Missouri, made tracks through this area, following ancient Native-American foot paths that became trails, which evolved into the roads we travel today.

       The Santa Fe Trail was a largely commercial route with traders traveling to and from for business and commerce. Few families traveled the Santa Fe Trail, unlike the Oregon and California Trails that developed in the 1840s and 1850s respectively.

Scene resembling Independence Square, ca. 1840s.

Many traders settled and established trading posts along the route. Some purchased lots around the Independence Square. For the pioneers this was a highly attractive location, being about three miles south of the Missouri River, with fresh water springs and plentiful timber. Store fronts began to dot the Square. The earliest structures were cabin-like buildings of hardwood logs hewn from trees felled on-site. Very soon, however, local brick manufacturing allowed for larger and more permanent structures to begin dominating the commercial blocks immediately around the Square.

Former Historic Preservation Manager Patrick H. Steele, Sr., wrote:

"In frontier towns like Independence, many of the earliest and finest permanent buildings were erected to house commercial and institutional enterprises. Businesses were intentionally clustered in a central district that would serve as the hub for town activities…. The individuality of the stores, offices, banks, and hotels…served not only as an advertisement for the business within, but also as a direct reflection of the proprietor's expertise…. Accordingly, storefronts have always been directly associated with myths about progress and change, and especially about the need to change appearance in order to stay competitive. The history of America's commercial architecture has become a history of remodeling, and the architecture of the historic Independence Square offers no exception to the rule."[13]

The Jackson County Courthouse had a permanent presence on Independence Square from the very beginning.

1831 Courthouse

Soon after the 1827 Log Jackson County Courthouse was completed, discussions began to build a more suitable brick and stone courthouse for the center of town.

During the November 1827 term the County Court commissioned a new, 12-window, two-story brick courthouse. It was to be 30-feet-long and 40-feet-wide, according to Lilburn W. Boggs, clerk of the County Court. The first floor was to have 12-foot ceilings and the second floor was to be 10-feet tall. Four chimneys were to be installed in each corner of the building so they could serve as fireplaces on both floors and accommodate logs four-feet-long in the first story, and three-feet in the second. The project was estimated to cost $1,500.

County Court minutes show that the brick and stone work was done by William Silvers, George H. Arnold and Eli Roberts for $799; that Samuel Weston did the carpentry work for $415; William Bowers furnished the lumber for $192.77; and, Levi Sheppard provided 10,000 shingles and other pieces of wood for $40.20.[14]

Work on the foundation began in 1828. By October 27, 1828, superintendent Lilburn W. Boggs reported that the foundation was finished and the brick walls were up about nine feet on the lower floor.[15] "Construction went slowly and there were problems on every hand, including the failure of William Bowers to fulfill his contract for planking. He was later sued. By June 13, 1829, Boggs was on the defensive and reporting that the brick work was "about two or three feet above the first

Lilburn W. Boggs

story," and was strong and substantial though "not as neat as it might have been, and the brick is as good as any that have been made or used in this part of the country...." He stated citizens had promised to pay for painting and penciling the outside walls, and for some extra work designed to add strength to the building. As proof of the durability of the walls, superintendent Boggs said that "a part of the work was completed last fall and yet stands good." Winter apparently had come before the building could be enclosed."[16]

"By August 3, 1829, Samuel Weston, the carpenter contractor, was busy inside, and William Blanton was ready with the six timbers for support of the second floor. Weston was to plane, or mill these timbers[17] and eventually eight were used. On August 2, 1830, Samuel Sweet was paid for filling in with brick around the 24 windows and two doors, and for laying two hearths.[18] Near the end of construction Boggs was replaced as Superintendent of Public Buildings by Jacob Gregg, June 27, 1831."[19]

The building was completed between September and October 1831. The County Court sold the 1827 Log Courthouse (and lot), as previously mentioned, on February 6, 1832. The 1831 building was soon found to have been improperly constructed and suffered maintenance problems from the start.[20] Because of its embarrassing history and short-lived use, most previous historical accounts do not even recognize this Jackson County Courthouse on Independence Square, and no images of the structure are known to exist.

The structure foundered and the County Court was forced to order construction of a completely new building. It had previously been thought that some foundational rock was re-used. As will be seen, even the foundation was sold.

On December 19, 1836, the County Court acknowledged receipt of a document from the Grand Jurors which described, "the dilapidated, deplorable condition of the courthouse," and the propriety of disposing of it and erecting a new one. It was felt that attempts at repairs would be "fruitless and unavailing."[21] The Court ordered building Superintendant, Henry Chiles, "to dispose of the courthouse now in use."

18

1838 Courthouse[22]

The County Court then ordered "that a new courthouse be built upon the site now occupied by the old one, and do appropriate the sum of five thousand dollars...."[23]

On February 6, 1837, the Jackson County Court ordered "that the foundation of the old courthouse be sold by the Superintendant [Henry Chiles]."[24]

On February 20, 1837, the Jackson County Court clerk, Samuel Combs Owens, recorded:

"Whereas, it has become necessary and expedient to erect a new courthouse in this county; and the County Court of this county having authorized the building of the same; and as it is intended to erect such a building for the said courthouse as shall be a credit to the county and not inferior to any in the adjoining counties, and

"Whereas, said house will cost a very considerable sum of money to be paid out of the county treasury, and

"Whereas, also, many citizens of this county have expressed a readiness and willingness to aid by private subscription or contribution in defraying the expense of erecting such a house;

"Therefore, the court doth order that William W. Kavanaugh, Samuel White, James Chiles, Thomas H. Talley, William Williams, and Robert C. Gwinn be and they are hereby appointed to receive subscriptions and contributions to aid in defraying the expense of building said courthouse and they are hereby requested to

Samuel C. Owens

use their exertions in procuring such subscriptions and contributions for this purpose. All sums received by them for this purpose shall be turned over to Henry Chiles, superintendent of the said courthouse, on or before the first day of October, next; and it is further ordered that each member of this commission be furnished with a copy of this order."[25]

No record of such subscriptions has been located. The County, however, borrowed from its "Road and Canal Fund" to rebuild the courthouse which was completed in September 1838.[26] By January 8, 1840, "six common chairs" were ordered for use by the Jackson County Court.[27] A lightning rod was ordered in May 1841 and installed in February 1842.[28] In July 1844, the County Court ordered sidewalks to the east door of the courthouse, and stone steps on the east and west entrances. The following month, the Court directed, "*John S. Lucas be and hereby employed by the Court to take care of the courthouse yard, to keep the gates closed, and keep out stock, for the space of one year for which attention the Court appropriates the sum of nineteen dollars payable at the expiration of the term.*"[29]

1838 Courthouse by Hermann Meyer, drawn in 1852.

20

A tall, thin, sharp-pointed spire was added in 1846, the year the ill-fated, 250-wagon Donner party left Independence Square for California. It was visible for miles in every direction on the pioneer landscape for the next six years. Of course, it didn't hurt that Independence Square situates on very high ground, about 800-feet above sea level.[30]

We are fortunate to have an 1852 view of this courthouse, drawn by a German tourist, Hermann Meyer, and later published in his 1857 German-language publication, "Meyer's Universum," where he wrote:

"From one of the oldest cities in Europe's central Alps [the preceding article was about the city of Chur, often called the oldest city in Switzerland] we now re-direct our gaze to the furthest frontier of European culture, in the North-American state of Missouri. Once the traveler has survived the difficult and dangerous steamboat trip up the great meanders of the Missouri River and after passing the former Fort Osage, he finally arrives at Wayne City, a place notorious for its devastating heat and also the landing for Independence. The distance by road from the Missouri to Independence is about four miles. Ten or twelve miles beyond Independence along the Santa Fe Trail lie the last farms on the edge of the vast prairie, and several days' journey further the trail to Oregon separates from the trail to New Mexico and Chihuahua, which we described on page 25 of this volume.

"Its location made this city what it is to this day—an important border and provisioning place that enjoys a persistently vibrant commerce providing the needs of trading and emigrant wagon trains, all of which formerly departed from here for New Mexico, Utah, California, and Oregon. In fact, the entire commerce of the "Plains" was formerly conducted in Independence. Today that distinction is disputed by Westport, which lies twelve miles further up the Missouri, and also by Fort Leavenworth, Weston, Saint Joseph, Council Bluffs, and Kanesville, although Independence still dominates. Consequently, this little city is extraordinarily lively during certain seasons. When the crowds of California emigrants assemble here, life and trade in the streets and outlying areas resembles a continual rural fair; the California wagon trains assemble at the city's edges. The city appears surrounded by a mobile fortification of wagons since it is there, in great workshops, that all the wagons are built which will carry the emigrants and their possessions

through the thousand miles of wilderness. Trade in mules and oxen is therefore also most important there.

"In 1852, Independence and its surrounding area has 4000 inhabitants, which support seven churches and nearly as many denominations. The Methodists have separated into southern and northern groups, which quote the Bible in support of, and in opposition to, slavery. The poor Negroes, as Southern Methodists, actually hear sermons in support of slavery!—Our illustration takes us into the center of the city where the appearance of ladies on horseback and wagons of all kinds provide a view of street life at the current furthest reach of human emigration." [31]

For years it was thought the 'front' of the courthouse was on Main Street, and that Meyer's view was looking directly west. However, the latest and best research has determined that the traditional 'front' of the courthouse is Lexington Avenue, and that Meyer's view is looking directly north. Meyer's engraving has been the study for other artists depicting Independence Square. Walter de Maris painted, "Gateway to the West" (later re-titled "The Westward March of America") in 1946 for the Trails Day celebration of Independence. This painting is in the collection of the State Historical Society of Missouri. Also, muralist Charles Goslin used the 1838 Courthouse as the centerpiece of his 2001-2002 painting, "Trails Leaving Independence," which hangs in the permanent gallery of the National Frontier Trails Museum.

A wooden fence encircled the building and its one and one-fourth acres of ground. But, that did not stop all unwanted traffic onto the lawn…or into the building, as was noted above. *"In the old days the care taken of the county courthouse building was not so good and sometimes the doors were left standing overnight. In cold weather, the town hogs got into the habit of sleeping in the room used by the County Court. As a result, the room became infested with fleas and when the time came for the spring term of court the judges found it impossible to give their complete attention to business because of the annoying pests. One of the judges hit upon a solution. A flock of sheep were confined overnight in the courtroom and the fleas jumped at the chance to reside in the luxury of the sheep's fleece. The next day not a flea could be found in the courtroom and the judges were left free to transact the public business in peace and dignity."* [32]

Oregon, California, and Mormon Trails Developed

Commercial traffic along the Santa Fe Trail continued, and it was heavily used during the Mexican War between 1846 and 1848 as military supplies were transported from the Missouri River towns like Independence to the Southwest.

Famed pioneer, Ezra Meeker (on left), in Independence when re-tracing in 1910 his 1852 trek west.

Another migration pattern began to emerge, when the first migrant train was organized at Independence to take missionaries to the northern Pacific Coast. "Missionaries Marcus and Narcissa Whitman in 1843 guided the first 'Great migration' to the West by leading a wagon train of 1,000 pioneers from Independence...to Oregon, where they had been since 1836. The 1841 Bidwell Bartleson party and the 1846 expedition of Colonel Alexander Doniphan brought attention to Spanish California and territory that became known as the American Southwest."[33] Expeditions and trail blazing continued through the 1840s as families seeking newly opened lands in Oregon and California Territories, and Mormons seeking religious freedom in Utah, funneled through Independence and Jackson County . . . and other points up the Missouri River.

Perhaps the most infamous wagon train of some 250 wagons leaving Independence Square was the ill-fated Donner Party of 1846. Their history is well-documented, as are other diarists, in the Merrill J. Mattes Research Library of the National Frontier Trails Museum located in Independence, Missouri.

Until 1854, travelers crossing the western Missouri border just a few miles west of Independence found themselves outside the political boundaries of the United States. That is, there were no states to the west of Missouri . . . only vast U.S. territories known collectively as the "Great American Desert," or "Indian Territory."

Independence Square merchants outfitted residents and travelers with the goods and services needed. Immediately around the Square was a business center of general mercantile stores, banks, hotels, and saloons. The County Jail also maintained a prominent presence in the midst of the hustle and bustle of day-to-day activity; it has always been located on one of the first two lots just south of present-day Truman Road and Main Street.

A second-tier of manufacturing businesses developed in the outlying blocks in every direction with livery stables, blacksmith shops, etc. The Robert Weston blacksmith shop, John G. McCurdy blacksmith shop, and the Hiram Young blacksmith shop each staked claims to fame in outfitting travelers with high-quality wagons, ox yokes, and other necessities for successful overland journeys. Young was also a noted, early, Independence resident of African descent. He saved his meager

24

earnings and secured his freedom from slavery, and then purchased his wife so she could also be free.

Imagine the excitement and trepidation overlanders felt as they gathered last-minute supplies in Independence and waited until winter had passed and the grasses on the plains were mature enough to sustain their livestock. They had come from all points east and had either traveled overland, or up the Missouri River, landing at Blue Mills or Wayne City Landing, making their way to the Square. Before them lay a 6-month journey across the continent once they 'jumped off' from Missouri's western boundary. Even more interesting is that emigrants did not ride in wagons as portrayed in Hollywood movies. Without wagon seats or shocks, people walked the 2,000+mile journey through the late spring and summer months each year.

McCurdy Blacksmith and Carriage Shop.

Try to picture Independence Square in the spring and summer of 1849 after gold had been discovered at John Sutter's place in California Territory. Some 5,000 to 6,000 wagons left Missouri that spring. Sutter had been a mercantile owner in the border town of Westport, Missouri (today, a retail shopping district in Kansas City, Missouri).

When artist Alfred S. Waugh visited Independence in 1845 he wrote, *"In the center of a small square, enclosed in a wooden fence, stands a low, square, two story brick court house.... Around are a number of irregular buildings used by small traders and dignified with the lofty sounding title of stores. At present a Mr. Wood Noland, or Uncle Wood as he is familiarly known, is building a large house at S W corner of the square which he intends to occupy as a hotel."*[34] Waugh was invited to set up his easel in the courthouse by General Samuel D. Lucas, who then introduced his friends to the artist where he "commenc[ed] opperations

Captain John Augustus Sutter

[sic.] in face making." Waugh wrote, *"The first likeness I made was of the general, it was in the new style, and gave so much satisfaction that sitters came in sufficiently fast, to allow us to make some outlay for our comfort."*[35]

The summer of 1850 saw an even larger emigration where it is estimated that more than 50,000 emigrants traveled west.[36] Towns in Jackson County struggled to supply travelers with the goods they needed to survive the journey. Independence Square was undoubtedly a hopping place with all kinds of activity . . . and some unruly behavior.

Samuel D. Lucas by Alfred S. Waugh

1853 Courthouse[37]

Commonly recorded history relays that Mexican War veterans returning to Jackson County in 1848 found the courthouse enlarged in all four directions and newly resurfaced in a modified Greek Revival-style. However, recent research into Jackson County Court records has documented this enlargement as taking place between June 1852 and May 1853.[38]

In June 1852, Jacob C. Hovey and John McCoy were appointed as commissioners to provide a plan for enlarging and improving the courthouse. The following month the County Court accepted the low bid from the firm of Leonard and Stewart for $12,500. Early in 1853, parts of the building were ready. By May, the work was completed.[39]

In the earliest days of the Jackson County Courthouse, local church congregations that lacked gathering spaces were permitted to use the Circuit Court room. "When the courtroom was used in this manner, the judge's bench was the pulpit, the choir could have sat in the jury box, and congregants huddled near the fireplaces."[40]

The square footage of the courthouse increased slightly in 1853, with the new walls enclosing its

1853 Courthouse by A. Ruger 1868 *Bird's Eye View of Independence, Missouri.*

predecessor. The balanced, symmetrical façade was modified by adding columned entry porches on the north and south, and evenly spaced, simple pilasters that projected slightly from all four walls.

The wooden fence previously encircling the Courthouse Square acreage was removed and replaced with what is thought to have been a simple iron enclosure.

A stunted, domed cupola atop a low-pitched hip roof replaced the prominent 1846 spire.

Westward travelers on the trails across Indian Territory to California, Oregon (and other states as they joined the Union), continued to pass by the Jackson County Courthouse. In the mid- to late 1850s, William McCoy, the first mayor of Independence in 1849, operated the banking company of Stone, McCoy & Company out of spaces in the courthouse. He later occupied the McCoy Bank building on the southwest corner of West Lexington Avenue and Liberty Street. During the Civil War it became the habit of the banking company doing business in the courthouse to bring its gold deposits over to the McCoy vault for safekeeping. Although McCoy's Bank building was used as Buell's headquarters during the First Battle of Independence, and sustained heavy artillery fire, no mention about lost deposits has yet been found.[41] It is also interesting to note that official County records were spared.

The Jackson County Courthouse was also requisitioned during the Civil War. Soldiers were quartered inside. It was used as a field hospital, and endured bullets fired in two major battles that raged through Independence Square, not to mention other skirmishes during the Border War and Civil War period, 1854-1864.[42] The courthouse suffered damage by the command under Colonel Jennison's regiment of Kansas Volunteers in November 1861; by Colonel Burris in August 1862 during the First Battle of Independence, when afterwards 19 or 20 wounded soldiers were moved to the courthouse for care; and, by Colonel Penick between September 1, 1862, and June 13, 1863. On July 6, 1863, Frederick F. Yeager, Miles Washington Burford, and James C. Carpenter, were appointed by the County Court as commissioners to assess damages to the courthouse, fencing and lawn. They reported much damage including the destruction of chairs, tables, stands, doors, windows, plastering, etc., to the extent of $510.90. Additionally, 70-feet of cobblestone and 902-feet of railing would cost another $4,138.[43] In April and May 1864, the Court replaced window panes and repaired the courthouse roof and dome.[44]

At the close of the "War Between the States," the County Court paid Peter Hinters $28 on March 20, 1865, to clean the landscape surrounding the courthouse.[45]

1853 Courthouse Square from northeast, by A. Ruger. The 1859 Jackson County Jail at bottom right has numeral "2" in the fenced, rear courtyard.

Years later, in 1908, Jackson County received "$410 rental for the courthouse and jail in Independence occupied by soldiers in war time.... The original [war] claim filed by the Jackson County officials amounted to $21,684. It was based upon the fact that about November 1, 1861, Union troops under Colonel Jennison took possession of the Independence Courthouse, the jail and Square upon which those buildings stood and

29

occupied them as officers' quarters and for hospital purposes. Other troops under the command of Colonel Buell, Colonel Van Horn, Colonel Penick and others occupied the buildings until July 1865. The claim was itemized as follows: Rent of the courthouse and Square, three years eight months and 14 days at $3,000 a year, $11,116; rent of jail from January 1, 1862, to July 15, 1865, at $720 a year, $2,548; repairs to buildings made necessary by reason of such occupancy, $8,000; total, $21,664."[46]

Artist A. Ruger visited Independence and ascended in a dirigible to capture a bird's eye view of the town in 1868. It shows two views of the 1853 Jackson County Courthouse on Independence Square. And, artist George Burnett studied this view of Independence Square for his painting titled, "Second Battle of Independence."

The walls of the 1853 Courthouse largely survive today; its walls define the east-south-west hallway surrounding the 1838 Courthouse.

George Burnett's rendition of the Second Battle of Independence, 1864. Jackson County Courthouse Square is in the distance.

1872 Courthouse

A burgeoning post-Civil War reconstruction boom saw Kansas City overtake Independence as the leading city in Jackson County. Kansas City's sharp population increase, land annexations and the associated real estate boom in the county's western range necessitated larger quarters for the proper functioning of Jackson County government.

Duplicate quarters for Jackson County government were instituted in Kansas City at this time (although Independence remains today the official, "County Seat").

In 1870, the Jackson County Court purchased the partially-completed Nelson House Hotel on the northeast corner of 2nd and Main Streets in Kansas City. The Nelson House Hotel was designed by noted Kansas City architect, Asa Beebe Cross, who also designed the 1859 Jackson County Jail and Vaile Mansion in Independence.

1872 Courthouse (from southeast)

The foundations for the Nelson House Hotel had been laid in 1869, and were "finished up" by action of the County Court in 1871.[47]

Also in 1872, $48,000 was expended to resurface the Independence Courthouse with red brick into a Second Empire style.

A clock tower was added for the first time. The clock tower was an extended, square, east wing featuring a concave mansard-topped tower with pointed belfry.

An iron balustrade and Grecian urns surrounded the adorned cornices of the roofline. In 1932, a newspaper report indicated that two of those urns were then at the home of John A. Sea, while and other urns adorned local homes, too.[48]

Two-story, ornate balconies and classical pediments were built on the north and south entrances. An iron fence surrounded the landscaped perimeter. In 1874, while Robert Weston caused a law to be passed preventing citizens from tying their horses to the trees surrounding the courthouse. The day following enactment of this law, Mr. Weston rode uptown, and as usual, tied his horse to the same old tree; consequently paying the first fine under the new law.[49]

In 1877, the County Court awarded a contract to W. H. Pollard to paint the Circuit Court courtroom and a separate contract to C. W. Fairman to "repair the dome of the courthouse."[50]

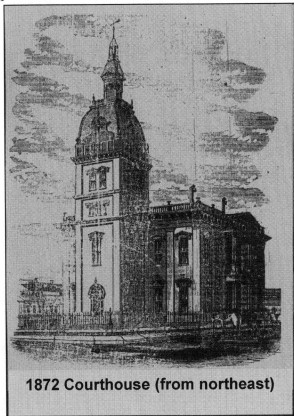

1872 Courthouse (from northeast)

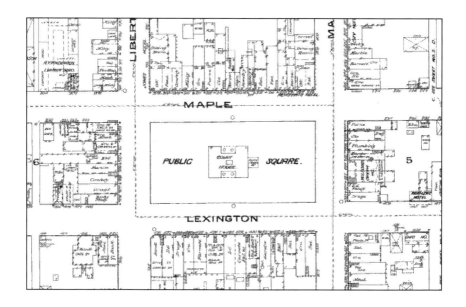

The above map is a Sanborn Fire Insurance map from August 1885. The view shows the Independence Square with the Courthouse situated in the middle of what is clearly more of a rectangle than a Square.

The footprint of the Courthouse building clearly shows the inset of the north and south entrances, which were sheathed in subway tile. Remnants of the first-floor tiled entranceways are visible today in the Visitor's Experience Center where architects created windows in the ceilings to reveal these architectural elements.

Of additional interest are the outlines of buildings surrounding the historic Square, which in 1885, were most likely first- and second-generation structures dating to the Square's origin in the late 1820s.

1887 Courthouse and 1889 Annex

In 1887, to streamline building maintenance issues, certain ornamentation was removed to give the building a more modern and less Victorian look. The millwork and ornamental limestone fretwork that provided architectural interest—but which were not structurally significant—were stripped from the façade.

The names of the County Court judges at that time, John A. McDonald, Hugh Lynch, and William C. Chiles, were inscribed in the sandstone cornerstone.

This artifact survived the remodeling work done in 1907 and 1933. It was re-set in the east basement wall during the 1933 expansion. It can be seen today (2013) in the

1887 dedicatory plaque.

Recorder of Deeds' offices on the lower level of the courthouse.

The clock tower wing was enlarged for office space and the 6-foot tall clock face was painted black with gilded Roman numerals. Another notable exterior change was a porch that was added to the east entrance. On August 7, 1932, the *Kansas City Star* reported that the 1887 pillars at the entrance to the clock tower had been re-purposed at the home of Samuel H. Woodson at 1604 West Lexington Avenue (now Winner Road).

1887 Courthouse (from northeast)

In Kansas City that same year (1887), construction began on a new Jackson County Courthouse that took up the city block between 5th and Missouri, and Oak and Locust Streets. Patterned after the State House in Denver, Colorado, it was opened in 1892. In 1887, the Missouri General Assembly passed a law setting forth the terms "where county courts are now or may hereafter be held at more places than one, and at other places than the county seat."[51] This applied specifically to the Jackson County Court, and any Missouri county containing 75,000 or more inhabitants.

36

This allowed the County Court to hold its sessions in Kansas City or Independence.

A $35,000 annex was built adjacent on the west in 1889, connecting to the 1887 Courthouse by an iron bridge, or sky walk, from the second floor.[52] This annex continued to serve through 1932.

Two views showing portions of the 1889 Annex. Left: looking from the north.

Right: Looking from the southwest corner towards Maple Avenue.

Also in 1889, a basketball-sized granite spherical marker was placed on the lawn of the County Courthouse:

City Datum
Elevation
326 and   74/100 feet
1889
P. H. Grinter, C.E.

Workers removed the elevation marker prior to construction in 2009; it is reinstalled at the southeast corner of the Courthouse.

If the courthouse is about 800-feet above sea level, how can the 326 and 74/100 feet be accurate? Grinter, who was County Highway Engineer in 1889, said the marble ball marked the elevation above low water mark on the Hannibal Bridge in Kansas City, which was indicated on the bridge by a copper bolt. Grinter said the city "datum" was merely a bench mark for the use of surveyors.[53]

In 1897, the Independence Courthouse had a new timepiece installed, and at some point an 1879-vintage bell salvaged from a Missouri River steamboat was installed in the belfry. The bell, which was silent for many years in the 1990s and early 2000s due to mechanical issues, now tolls as a remnant and reminder of the countless hours that have transpired in our vibrant history.[54]

Three decorative, stained glass windows were placed in the north side of the Circuit Court courtroom in September, 1906. They depict the official seals of the State of Missouri, Jackson County, and the City of Independence. The courtroom later became known as the "Brady Courtroom," and comprises the upper floor of the original 1838 Courthouse. See the biographical highlight about Brady below.

"For several years the big arrow on the top of the courthouse spire [had] been in a state of collapse.... The Mize Hardware Company was given the contract in March 1904 to make repairs.[55]

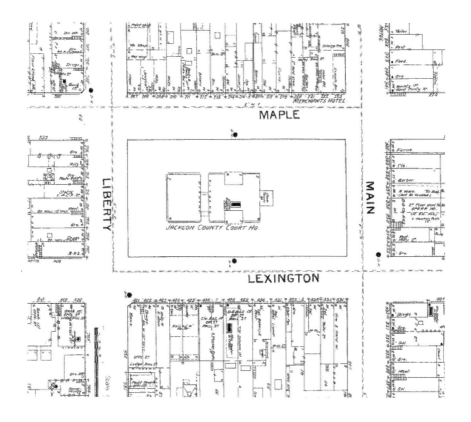

The above drawing is a Sanborn Fire Insurance map from December 1892. The view shows the Independence Square with the Courthouse situated in the middle, much like the earlier map from 1885.

The main difference in the footprint of the building between 1885 and 1892 is the annex situated to the west of the main building, and connected by the aforementioned bridge, or sky walk. The Courthouse on the September 1898 edition of the Sanborn map is identical to the 1892 edition.

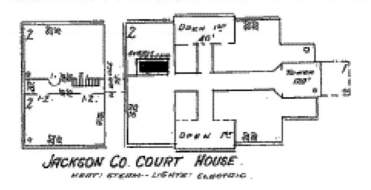

JACKSON CO. COURT HOUSE

The floor plan shown above is an extract from the Sanborn Fire Insurance map from September 1907.

The footprint in this view is more detailed than earlier versions of Sanborns in that the interior hallways are defined. A stairwell is depicted in the 1889 annex. In the main building, a large, darkened, rectangular area is marked "Steam Heater." The north and south entrances are delineated as "Open." And, the "120' Tower" is noted on the east end.

The 1889 annex served through 1932 when it was razed during extensive building renovations.

1907 Courthouse

Bids were received by the County Court on May 26, 1906, to remodel the lower floor of the Jackson County Courthouse on Independence Square, and for raising the height of the tower.

1907 Courthouse (north/east)

General revenue funds in the amount of $100,000 were used to raise and restyle the Second Empire tower.[56] William E. Brown was selected as the architect.[57]

The 1872 black clock faces were retained. However, the movement was destroyed during installation when a 1,500-pound clock weight snapped from its cable, ripping through two joists on its descent. A clock mechanism was recycled from the City of Independence. Local jeweler, C. W. Fuchs, was contracted by the County Court to put the city clock in the courthouse tower.[58]

North and south entranceways were enclosed, expanding the upstairs courtroom. See Brady Courtroom chapter for additional details.

The entire building was resurfaced to cover crumbling red bricks with buff-colored brick. Also, the 1872 iron fence surrounding the courthouse lawn was removed. Work was completed in 1907.[59]

Everett Miller, former head custodian of the courthouse, said that the bell rang all night to celebrate the Armistice of World War I in 1919, as did all the church bells in town. *"There was excitement on the Square that night,"* he recalled. *"People were parading around, some were hollering and whooping, and shot guns were fired. People really carried on."*[60]

1933 Historic Truman Courthouse

The 1907 Courthouse on Independence Square served Jackson Countians 25 years until they, at the beginning of the Great Depression, passed a multimillion-dollar public works bond issue that allotted $200,000 for a new County Courthouse on Independence Square.

**Artist/architect's concept design rendering
by David Frederick Wallace, 1932.**

"As the highest elected official in the County of Jackson, Judge [Harry S.] Truman provided the leadership not only to pave thousands of miles of roads [and build bridges] but to provide improvements to the Independence Square Courthouse and to construct a new 15-story courthouse in downtown Kansas City in the style of the times, Art Deco. He took a prominent interest in the courthouse renovation in Independence. He traveled the country studying the architecture of other public building and talking to architects at his own expense and on his own time. It was at Judge Truman's direction and insistence that the core of the [1838] Courthouse structure remain."[61]

"When the 1907 building was vacated for remodeling, a free, public dance was held in the building."[62]

One of the persons who personally vouched for the "historic treasure" was Dwight Brown, Kansas City Architect. Brown, as a young professional just out of college, labored on the complicated rehabilitation project in 1932-1933.

Brown was working with David Frederick Wallace (Bess Truman's uncle), whose special interest, talent, and training were in colonial architecture. Wallace's concept of design was the one from which the courthouse architectural firm, Keene and Simpson, made the working drawings.

According to Brown, there were no blueprints of the 1838 Courthouse and they could find no working drawings of the 1887 remodeling.

The County Court had voted to raze all of the structure, save the 1838 original, Brown said. In actuality, this was not done, as portions of previous remodelings were salvaged and incorporated into the 1933 design. Demolition was required of at least the east portion that supported the square clock tower that had been added in 1872.

Brown said his assignment was to make a drawing of the nearly century-old unit (at that time). *"I measured the old building inside and out—every wall, partition and beam,"* Brown said. *"I can testify to its antiquity."* Brown recalled that some of the beams were joined with wooden pegs and that the plaster was "horse hair" vintage. *"Wallace drew his plans to enclose the [1838] unit,"* Brown added.

44

The buff brick facing that had given the courthouse a new look in 1907 was removed. Red colonial brick and white Indiana limestone trimmings were added to punctuate classical columns and porticos on the north and south. In "Survivors: A Catalog of Missouri's Remaining 19th Century County Courthouses," author J. Bradley Pace described the end-result of the 1933 remodeling as, *"a pleasing and elegant structure inspired by Independence Hall and resembling a Colonial Virginia meetinghouse."*

The seal of the State of Missouri can be found above the north portico, and the seal of Jackson County above the south portico.

Above the east and west entrances stone reliefs of an American eagle surrounded by a wreath symbolize victory and progress.

The 1872-vintage black clock faces were painted white. Carl Dimoush remembers seeing the old black clock faces in the shop of his grandfather, William Dimoush, who operated the Dimoush Planing Mill (formerly Stewart-Dimoush) in Independence.[63] The faces were re-installed and accented with 14-inch-long black Roman numerals. These were incorporated into the new 45-feet-high, 15-feet square cupola.

Below, the Dimoush Planing Company vehicle.

What you don't see from the outside is that, "the Independence Hall patterned clock tower is supported by the center core of the original structure, which was 40 by 30 feet," Brown said in an article appearing in the March 1974 *Jackson County Historical Society JOURNAL*. In fact, remnants of two former courthouse roof tops are also still partially visible in the attic. For more details, see the "Brady Courtroom" chapter that follows.

Massive wood beams were added to support the centralized clock tower (above).

To the right: steel beams rest upon brick pillars that press firmly down onto the 1838 nucleus of the building.

47

**Jackson County Truman Courthouse clock tower belfry,
with the 1879 steamboat bell at the very top of the cupola.**

Another relict from the past, the 1879 steamboat bell, was retained. Printed reports gathered over the years indicate there were periods—long periods—when the bell would cease tolling. In 1975, County Public Works verified that an old bell about two and a half feet across was at the top of the cupola. There was no clapper in the bell, but attached to a rope was a 10-pound metal striker, or metal hammer arm which struck the edge of the bell.

"The bell will chime again, on the hour. *'The sound is beautiful. It's got a great tone to it,"* said Jackson County Executive, Mike Sanders.[64]

Inside the clock tower remains the original clockworks, which due to the cost in maintenance, have been updated with an electronic mechanism. The ladder to the rear leads straight up to the belfry. In the recent restoration, spray foam was added between the studs for insulation.

Maxine Moore Boardman, who grew up in Independence, said her father, Earl Moore, was an architectural engineer who was one of the contractors on the 1933 remodeling. Her grandfather, Frederick Kochler, was a jeweler on the 2nd floor of a building across from the courthouse on the north side of the Square. Koehler used to climb the clock tower and wind the clock every day, according to Boardman. She also noted that Koehler ran for Vice President of the United States on Eugene V. Deb's ticket.[65]

Truman and the Jackson County Court were successful in their 10-year public works program. They promoted their achievements and future planning projections to fellow County Court commissioners in other Missouri counties and surrounding states through a book titled, "Results of County Planning". This book contains stunning views, all captured by local photographer, Dick Millard, under the direction of Truman, who traveled with Millard around Jackson County to gather the images presented in the book.

Their 'county planning' was so forward-thinking that it even contained formative ideas for future county parks and man-made lakes. More than 20-years-later, local voters approved a bond issue to create and develop Lake Jacomo (which stands for 'Jackson County Missouri') that officially opened May 30, 1959. The "Results of County Planning" document projected another lake that became Longview Lake, which was opened in 1986.

The Jackson County Court, 1927. Seated: Robert W. Barr; Harry S. Truman; Howard J. Vrooman. Standing: Edwin Becker, Court Deputy; Fred Boxley, County Counselor.

On October 12, 1932, Harry S. Truman attended a road celebration barbeque at Sni-A-Bar Farm in Grain Valley, Missouri. Indeed, engineers had given, according to "Results of County Planning", "careful consideration to every phase of traffic needs, particularly the *trends of traffic* which must necessarily affect the convenience of coming generations."

From left to right: Thomas Bash, Judge, Western District, 1929-1930; Robert W. Barr, Judge, Eastern District, 1927-1930; Howard J. Vrooman, Judge, Western District, 1927-1928; Eugene I. Purcell, Judge, Eastern District, 1931-1932; Presiding Judge Harry S. Truman; W. O. Beeman, Judge, Western District, 1931-1932.

A Dedication 80 Years Ago
1933

When the new courthouse was dedicated on September 7, 1933, it incorporated remnants from the prior remodeled buildings, including the nucleus consisting of the 1838 first, permanent, brick Jackson County Courthouse, and most of its 1853 successor. This decision was made at the insistence of the then Presiding Judge of the Jackson County Court, Harry S. Truman. He said in his opening remarks, *"Here is your courthouse finished and furnished within the budget set aside to build it."*

It was an all day affair when an estimated 40,000 attended the celebration in 91 degree heat (without air conditioning). Square merchants installed special window displays and offered special sales on dedication day. The Independence Business and Professional Women's Club were hostesses of a luncheon at the Independence Country Club for dignitaries that included Missouri Governor Guy B. Park, who delivered the afternoon keynote address:

"This stately structure, graceful in its architecture, yet portraying strength, and modern in all of its appointments, is a fine monument to the thrift, energy and progressiveness of the splendid citizenry of Jackson County.

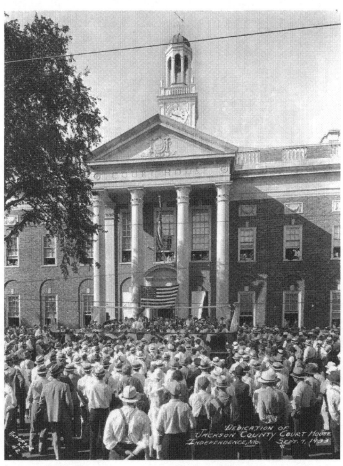

"It is appropriate that you are gathered in such large numbers to participate in these ceremonies. It is your courthouse and to you and the generations to follow it is dedicated in the name of Justice and for the preservation of your rights and liberties and the good order of citizenry.

"'Here the sovereign law, the expressed will of the people of our state, shall sit serenely on her throne....'"

"In this building may the chosen servants of your selection perform their duties and conduct your business with fairness, honesty and efficiency and practice that strict economy so essential to good government.

"While your pride in this building is becoming, it is well to remember that it is not populous cities with handsome buildings towering towards the skies, or factories vibrant with the busy hum of machinery, or broad paved highways stretching out in every direction, that makes Missouri great.

55

"It is her God-fearing, liberty-loving people that make her great, with the strength and courage to do right and to oppose wrong.

"Such were the hardy pioneers who more than a century ago settled here, felled the trees, and hewed the logs for your first courthouse. Many of you here today are the direct descendants of those brave and dauntless men and women.

"From this point first following the ox trains started across the plains, later riding swiftly by rail, the population moved ever westward, until now we are in the very heart of America. To quote from the late Champ Clark, 'In a state around whose borders could be constructed a

Chinese wall and her people live in comfort, so diversified are her resources.'

"While this is true and wonderful has been her progress during, but a little more than a century of statehood and great are her achievements, yet today we face a task equally as hard and dangerous and probably more grave and threatening than did our illustrious forebears.

"To meet the situation confronting us will require courage and sacrifice and will put to the test the strength of our manhood and womanhood. In the midst of our plenty came want and hunger.

DEDICATION OF JACKSON COUNTY COURT HOUSE INDEPENDENCE, MO. SEPT. 7, 1933

"Strong men, willing to work, cannot find employment and are wearily walking our streets and highways vainly searching for the wherewithal to feed their hungry children. Property tax has become an unbearable burden; business is stagnant. Factories and mines are closed and prices on farm products hit the bottom; we have been drifting, drifting, towards national calamity if not national collapse.

57

"My fellow citizens, in all seriousness I admonish you to fall in, shoulder to shoulder behind your chose leader. Put aside, for the time, all partisanship and selfishness and petty things, for neither politics nor religion or any other thing should come before patriotism. Emulate the fine example of your dauntless ancestors, who, a century ago suffered privation, hardship and want that you might have this beautiful city in which to dwell in comfort and happiness.

"It is not my nature to be an alarmist or to look into the future with despair, and I have not lost faith in the ability of the American people to govern themselves, but I am not unmindful of the wisdom of our motto, 'In union there is strength.' We must stand together in this cause."

The day-long festivities also included a motion picture show; Old Fiddlers' contest; swimming and diving contests at the Independence Natatorium; horse show and ladies' riding contest; a parade; band concerts; championship sports of all kinds; street dances; a carnival; and, a pageant depicting the historical development of Jackson County.

Rounding out the day was a pageant at the Soldiers' and Sailors' Memorial Building (today, the Truman Memorial Building) depicting the history of progress titled, "Century of Progress." The colorful and authentic pageant was written by Independence resident, Charles Blevins Davis, as part of the official courthouse celebration. More than 300 local persons took part in the production presented in eight episodes. Scenes depicting the Mexican War; Civil War, including a cabinet meeting of Abraham Lincoln, and the surrender of General Lee to General Grant, led up to the closing scenes depicting the World War I days and the formal dedication of the new Jackson County Courthouse.

Harry Truman's daughter, Miss Margaret Truman, and long-time Independence Mayor Roger T. Sermon, Sr., unveiled the official dedication tablets on the south side of the building.

Upstairs two paintings were dedicated in the Circuit Court courtroom. Independence resident and amateur artist, Fred F. Brightman, whose career was in the newspaper business, painted and donated two categorical paintings for the new courthouse that portray county and state history.[66]

Jackson's Mantle on the Blue

Brightman's painting, "Jackson's Mantle on the Blue," (on the left) "visualizes objects and incidents typifying the county which bears the famous president's name. [It] portrays Old Hickory in military costume worn at the Battle of New Orleans with a blue mantle draped about his shoulders.

"Hat in hand, he stands at the mouth of the Blue on Benton's rock, from which a legend says, 'Thomas Hart Benton, famed Missouri statesman, forecast a great future for this section of country.'

"In the right foreground the Centropolis Bridge across the Blue is pictured. Nearby are

Andrew Jackson

the tepees of Shugaw, the friendly Indian chief from whom Sugar Creek was named, and near them stands the old log cabin, Jackson County's first courthouse. Directly behind the log cabin is Bingham's tulip tree, planted by the famous Missouri artist at Miss Tillery's boarding school for young ladies....

"To the right is a hickory grove, symbolic of the Lee's Summit country. The course of the Blue is then traced to Horseshoe Lake where the new bridge at that point is portrayed. Then there is a wide expanse of fertile fields representative of the 'Sni' country. Historic standard oak in the Six-Mile community and the old black jack oak for which Lone Jack was named make up the right background of the painting. Jackson Stands with his right hand on, "Thirty Years in Congress," written by his one-time enemy, Thomas Hart Benton."

Jefferson's Seal in All Lands

The other Brightman painting is titled, "Jefferson's Seal in All Lands," and was said to be, "reminiscent of the life and deeds of the father of democracy." The artist portrayed, "Thomas Jefferson, third president of the United States, in the costume of Lafayette, his co-patriot." He is pictured looking into his seal, which contains his portrait and a French motto for the declaration of the rights of man, all inspired by his visit to France.

Thomas Jefferson

"At the time of Jefferson's visit there, Mr. Brightman says the French people had not been free from the yoke of despotism long enough to use their own initiative in putting into practice these principles. With these ideas, Jefferson returned to the United States prepared to write the Declaration of Independence.

"In his left hand, the artist pictured Jefferson holding the document of Independence up to his motto as if to say, "I have lived up to my motto." Jefferson's right hand rests on a globe signifying that his principles have gone around the world. The Louisiana Purchase made during his presidential term is outlined on the globe. The table holding the globe also contains a Bible and some other pamphlets.

"An old-fashioned mantelpiece is at his back, showing decorations of a Wedgewood plaque and a French lamp. A deep red curtain separates the figure of the man from views significant of his life and influence. At the top of the picture the snow-capped summits of the Colorado Mountains, one of the boundaries of the Louisiana Purchase, and the Hold Cross Mountain are sketched. The white columns are of the University of Missouri, which received a monument of Jefferson for being the first university in the Louisiana Purchase territory.

"Natural Bridge, in Virginia, which the famed president once owned and which he gave to the state, is also portrayed. The initials of George Washington adorn it. A house said to have belonged to Daniel Boone in Virginia as well as 'the winding wall' is also shown. In the right foreground is shown an old-fashioned basket of fruit, grapes and apples. The apples represent the Bellflower species, which Jefferson is credited with having introduced to this country."[67]

Over the years, the paintings' provenance forgotten, the artwork was taken down and stored in an unused area of the building. Judge Vernon E. Scoville, III, found them in a dilapidated state and invited students at the Kansas City Art Institute to do their best to restore them at no charge. Scoville then had them framed and re-mounted in the Circuit Court courtroom.

On September 4, 1933, a few days before the dedication, the Jackson County Court held its first session in the new courthouse. The only item of business that day, at the suggestion of the Court's record clerk, Edward H. Becker, was to instruct Rufus Burrus, assistant county counselor, to prepare an order re-designating the courthouse as the *official* place for the transaction of county business. This was necessary because during the remodeling and enlarging of the building the Court, under a similar order, had used the 1827 Log Jackson County Courthouse as the "official courthouse."[68]

1827 Log Jackson County Courthouse

Once the festivities were over it was back to business as usual . . . for another 30+ years.

Suburban Shopping
and Urban Renewal's Impacts
of the 1950s and 1960s

Business as usual has its ups and downs, naturally. Unfortunately, there were more downturns than upswings in the ensuing years for Jackson County's Courthouse Square.

The Independence Square thrived through the turn of the 19th century to the 1950s, where it was the center for social, commercial and cultural activities, as well as official county business. The Square remained vital to the community through two World Wars and the Korean War. It was closely connected to Kansas City neighborhoods and markets by a robust trolley/streetcar public transit system.

During the 1950's and 60's more and more suburban households acquired a second automobile. This provided the stay-at-home-spouse unprecedented freedom of mobility. The homemaker of the day, usually a woman, could now travel widely to shop for their family. This development and other factors had a devastating effect on the Square's retail district:

- Some Jackson County offices and courts left the courthouse to relocate three blocks away to the Eastern Jackson County Courthouse at 308 West Kansas Avenue, which was constructed in 1956 (and comprises the present-day east half of the building).[69] A $2 million addition on the west side of the Eastern Jackson County Courthouse was dedicated on May 1, 1972;

- Blue Ridge Mall, the Kansas City metropolitan area's first suburban shopping mall, opened in 1958, representing the rise of suburban shopping centers. It was initially an open air facility, but was later enclosed to provide an air conditioned environment;[70]

Blue Ridge Mall was the Kansas City metropolitan area's first suburban shopping mall, pictured here in the 1960s.

- On January 4, 1959, Kansas City's last trolley bus was pulled from service, signaling a definite disconnect between the age-old sister cities;[71]

- The next month, the City of Independence applied for a federal program of land redevelopment known as "Urban Renewal" that would, over 10-years, redevelop a 520-acre section of the city that included the Independence Square and environs;[72]

- Consumers were attracted to the convenience of newly constructed 'big box stores' and malls near their residential neighborhoods;

- Rock-bottom prices on cheap imported products and the rise of discount stores (and later 'dollar stores') further lured shoppers away from locally owned 'mom-and-pop' businesses; and,

- Free and plentiful parking at shopping centers enticed American automobile owners seeking one-stop-shopping experiences.

Independence Square and the Jackson County Courthouse were not alone in dealing with the decay of a traditional hometown, downtown central business district. As early as July 1967, County officials were contemplating what to do with "the old courthouse in Independence." Remodeling was an option. Converting it into an historical center was another idea floated at the time by former President Harry S. Truman.[73]

Urban renewal era on Independence Square.

The County Court created the Independence Courthouse Advisory Commission early in 1969, and the City of Independence applied for grant-in-aid programs instituted by the federal government. One of the grant programs provided for in the Housing Act of 1949 was for Urban Renewal. "In 1954, Congress amended the Act to require a Workable Program for Community Improvement."[74]

A resulting program was the Land Clearance for Redevelopment Authority (LCRA), which provides tax abatement and bond financing in urban renewal areas. The LCRA also has the power of eminent domain. It became involved in projects in Independence and other metro-wide cities, including Kansas City, Missouri, and Kansas City, Kansas. LCRA focused on two main areas in Independence. One was the "Northwest Parkway," comprising a neighborhood (called "The Neck") south of present-day Harry S. Truman Presidential Library and Museum (today, McCoy Park).

The other project area was then termed "Jackson Square," which consisted of those blocks surrounding Independence Square. The area was re-configured by closing off the short ends (Main and Liberty) and routing traffic one-way along Maple and Lexington Avenues.

Concrete fountains, concrete covered walkways along the sidewalks, and a concrete retaining wall around the courthouse were also installed.

In the end, all modifications except the latter were removed within a short time, as they severely restricted access to merchants around the Square.

In the midst of the Urban Renewal-era, Jackson County's Historic Truman Courthouse was added to the National Register of Historic Places in 1972. Its association with former President Truman; its status as the oldest building in Missouri to be continually used as a county courthouse; and, for its architectural significance as an example of the Georgian Revival style; all made it a worthy addition to the National Register. There are only two other courthouses in the United States nominated to the National Register because of an association with a U.S. President: Old State Capitol in Springfield, Illinois; and, Montgomery County Courthouse in Ohio, because of their association with President Abraham Lincoln.

Urban renewals' Jackson Square included a concrete
courtyard; concrete walkways closing off streets;
concrete fountains; and concrete covered walkways.

The images of Independence Square in this chapter are
the first and only two that have yet been donated to the
Jackson County Historical Society. Donations of original
photographs are welcomed for continued preservation
and future access to document this era of the Square.

Brady Courtroom

The Jackson County Circuit Court courtroom (today, the Brady Courtroom) as it appeared just after the 1933 remodeling when local photographer, Dick Millard, assisted the Jackson County Court in producing images for the book, "Results of County Planning."

Glimpses of the original 1838 Courthouse can be found within the current-day building (2013). An angled, first-floor closet in northwest quarter of the building (an employee break room as of 2013) reveals a remnant of one of the original, four-corner fireplace flues. Inside the Jackson County Historical Society's History Center, just to the left of its bookshop vault door, the southeast corner of the 1838 structure survives. One can stand at that corner and look out the current-day windows to see just how large the courthouse lawn was in those earliest days.[75]

The second-floor Circuit Court courtroom, commonly known as the Brady Courtroom, is the actual second-floor of the 1838 Courthouse, excluding the north side extension of the room. If the "battleship linoleum" —imported from Norway and installed throughout the building in 1967—were to be removed from this room, it might reveal the location where the original 1838 staircase originally connected the first- and second floors.[76]

Each of the four, angled corners of the room represents the location of one of the four original 1838 fireplaces. The exterior walls of the hallway surrounding the 1838 Courthouse are the 1853 Courthouse expansion.

In the basement a brick-lined tunnel runs beneath the early structure connecting the two ends of the current-day building.

Variation of Meyer's engraving of the 1838 Courthouse.

Three stained glass windows and an alcove were added to the Courtroom in 1906.

The left-hand pane depicts the Seal of the City of Independence (adopted in 1849); the right-hand window showcases the Seal of the County of Jackson (pictured to the left); and, the center window has a representation of the 1822 Seal of Missouri (enlarged below).

One visitor on tour asked, "Why does the State Seal have two polar bears?"

The brown bears have faded to white likely because they were fired improperly during the production process.

The three windows at the rear, or south side, of the Courtroom have let sun shine illuminate the room since 1838 when the Courtroom was first placed into service.

Imagine the thousands of court cases presented in this room between 1838 and 2001, when the last case was heard.

When Honorable Paul Vardeman toured the renovated courthouse in 2013, he shared a few tid-bits from his personal experience as a lawyer and later as a judge in the Brady Courtroom. He said, "Plaintiff, defendant and respective counsel always sat at one, large, wooden table, directly across from one another as their case was tried." He added with a chuckle, "A lawyer adept at reading upside down and backwards could learn to decipher his opponent's notes."

Vardeman said that the jury room was directly behind the jury box (pictured above). One problem was that the acoustics allowed their deliberations to sometimes be overheard, "which was often devastating to a lawyer," said Vardeman.

Below the judge's bench was a gun holster . . . just in case. There are no known instances of a judge needing to use a firearm in this room. However, an incident may have initiated the holster's installation.

Finally, Vardeman commented while on tour on the absence of spittoons in the Courtroom. He said, "There was a large spittoon sitting on a rug of sorts (to protect the battleship linoleum) at the north end of the table where the litigants sat. Lawyers had to be careful when circulating about the Courtroom or approaching the jury or witness boxes not to trip over the spittoon."

This oldest room in the building was used continuously from 1838 until June 1972 when Sixth District Magistrate Court Judge Joseph J. "Joe" Brady's court moved to the Eastern Jackson County Courthouse on Kansas Avenue. A report at that time said that the old courtroom had "been the scene of more than 125,000 civil and criminal hearings."[77] Magistrate Courts were established under a 1945 state law, and were the lowest of the state courts; but, the procedures were the same used in higher jurisdictions. Brady, a native of Independence, attended William Chrisman High School. He earned a law degree from the Kansas City School of Law, taking classes at night school while operating a grocery store by day.

Hon. Joseph J. Brady

Brady's first day with the Sixth District was on January 1, 1947. He enjoyed a 25+year tenure where he handled misdemeanors, civil suits up to $3,500 and preliminary hearings for felonies. "Delinquent notes, past due bills, petty thievery, evictions, felony arraignments, child support lapses, burglaries, wife beatings, trespass—criminal or civil—Joe Brady heard them all, with dignity and dispassion. He called them as he saw them," said Keith Wilson, Jr.

"He was the fairest judge that anyone could ever imagine," said Mrs. Arlene Marqua, clerk in Brady's courtroom for 25 years. "He always tried to judge others as he would himself if he were on the other side of the bench." The Sertoma Club gave Judge Brady its highest award for "Service to Mankind," and former President Harry S. Truman made the presentation. As a memorial and tribute to Judge Joseph J. Brady, the upstairs courtroom of the Historic Truman Courthouse became informally known as the "Brady Courtroom."[78] A portrait painted by Joseph Lewis, an Independence artist, was presented to the court in 1977. It hangs in a

73

prominent location over the jury box in the Division 30 Courtroom on the third floor of the Eastern Jackson County Courthouse at 308 West Kansas Avenue in Independence.

Hon. Vernon E. Scoville, III

The courtroom was unused from 1972 until the early 1990s when the Jackson County Legislature officially changed, by statute, the location of Division 104 from Kansas City to Independence. The Honorable Vernon E. Scoville, III, who was then officiating downtown, had discovered a huge backlogged docket for married couples seeking straightforward divorce cases. According to Scoville, his clerk suggested using Brady's former courtroom. Every other Friday beginning around September 1993, according to Judge Scoville, he would hear some 50+ cases. In about six months the docket was dwindled down. He continued to hear civil, criminal and jury cases. "Lawyers were fascinated trying cases here because it resembled a 'To Kill a Mockingbird' kind of courtroom," said Scoville. He added, "Because the building wasn't ADA compliant—without an elevator—in those days, if a litigant needed access to the Court and couldn't maneuver steps, we would simply move the court recorder downstairs and held court in Truman's old County Court courtroom."

Scoville, a graduate of the University of Missouri-Kansas City, served as an assistant Jackson County prosecutor then became an Assistant Public Defender and later a member of the Missouri House of Representatives before being appointed to the bench in 1991. O April 23, 2001, the Court discontinued use of the Jackson County Courthouse on Independence Square. On that day, Judge Scoville had all of the attorney's appearing before the Magistrate Court, Jackson County, Missouri District 4, Division 104, Division 28, sign their name, indicate the type of case they tried, and their Bar number on a commemorative roster.

During his years of tenure with Division 28 of the 16th Judicial Circuit Court in the Jackson County Courthouse on Independence Square, Judge Scoville was a passionate supporter and defender of the building even as county departments continued to relocate elsewhere. As was stated previously, he found two 1933 paintings and had them restored and mounted in the Circuit Court courtroom. Scoville retired June 28, 2013.

In later years before the courthouse was remodeled, the Brady Courtroom was occasionally used for documentary and short feature-film productions seeking an old courtroom: including "Last Will," starring Tatum O'Neal, James Brolin, Tom Berenger and Patrick Muldoon (filmed in November 2007; released online in 2010); "10-J: The History of the Federal Reserve Bank of Kansas City," produced by Kansas City Public Television (KCPT-Channel 19); and, KCPT's 90-minute documentary, "Bad Blood" (filmed in 2006; aired in 2007).

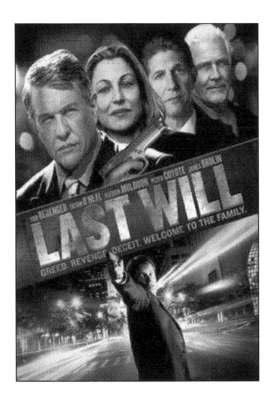

Elaborate millwork and plaster were added in the Victorian era.
The lamp is classic Art Deco from the 1933 remodeling.

Harry S. Truman's Office and Courtroom

Harry S. Truman began his career in elected politics in the Presiding Judge's office, and the Jackson County Court courtroom in the first floor, southeast section of the courthouse. In recognition of their historical significance, these spaces were saved from major changes over the years. They have now been restored to interpret Truman's headquarters when he worked as one of the County's highest elected officials.

Truman was first elected as Eastern District Judge for the County Court and served from 1922 to 1924. He was defeated for re-election in 1924 (the only election Truman ever lost); but, was elected Presiding Judge in 1926 and re-elected in 1930, serving on the Court until 1934.

The County Court was a three-member county legislative body that guided County government from 1827 through the early 1970s, when the form of government changed to today's Jackson County Legislature. The 'legislators' were then called 'county judges,' and might be likened to the 'county commissioner' position. If Truman were serving today his title would be "Jackson County Executive."

In Truman's day there was a "Western District Judge," who, in theory, represented and was elected from precincts in Kansas City; an "Eastern District Judge," representing eastern Jackson County; and a "Presiding Judge,"

**Harry S. Truman
around 1932**

77

who held an at-large position. Among other duties, the Presiding Judge served as a tie-breaker on delicate issues.

"Truman was a very active judge who pursued a policy of reform and capital improvements. He was never linked successfully to the corruption of the Pendergast machine. Instead, Truman campaigned on and apparently followed a policy of getting "an honest day's work" from patronage employees and awarding contracts to the lowest bidder, regardless of a contractor's political affiliation. These policies inspired enough public trust for Truman's Court to secure voter approval of a bond proposal to establish a county road network...for the Kansas City Courthouse and Jail [construction], Independence Courthouse remodeling and County Hospital improvements. The bond issue proposals were passed on May 8, 1927, Truman's birthday. By September the road program was underway."[79]

On a visit home from the White House for Christmas 1949, Truman dedicated and Margaret Truman unveiled the five-foot, bronze, equestrian statue of Andrew Jackson. The statue is an exact, but smaller replica of one Truman erected on the courthouse lawn in downtown Kansas City in 1934. The replica had been given to Truman by the sculptor, Charles Keck, but a lack of funds had postponed its setting at the courthouse on Independence Square.[80]

Andrew Jackson equestrian statue on Independence Square

Truman then went inside for the County Court's dedication of a portrait of Truman, which was installed in the County Court courtroom (now known as the Truman Courtroom). He stood behind his old chair used when he was Presiding Judge, and beneath a portrait bearing the following inscription:[81]

INDEPENDENCE, MO., TUESDAY, DECEMBER 27, 1949

PRESIDENT BACK IN FAMILIAR SPOT AT COURTHOUSE

Harry S. Truman, President of the United States, Judge of the County Court, Eastern District, 1922-1924, Presiding Judge, 1926-1934

On the President's right, Judge Harry M. Gambrel, then Presiding Judge. On Truman's left, Judge Fred W. Klaber, Western District Judge. Judge William Randall, Eastern District Judge, is at the left of the photograph.

The County's Parks and Recreation Department completed restoration of these spaces in August 1973, and included "undoing" work completed in the previous remodeling of the rooms in 1967.

The small office off the main corridor was used by the County Court secretary. In this room today are historical displays as well as the re-located IBM 'master clock' that once controlled each timepiece throughout the building, which were called, 'slaves.' The only 'slave' remaining today is in the adjoining room in the County Court courtroom. This clock was disconnected from the 'master' and stopped in December 1972 when President Truman passed away. This was in deference to Mr. Truman, as it was a mourning custom with people in his generation to stop clocks from ticking and place black cloth over mirrors.[82]

Recollections of Agnes Fraher Biter, Judge Truman's personal secretary, and Everett Miller, building custodian at the time when Truman worked there, were instrumental in the restoration. Others assisted in locating and donating artifacts to help interpret the spaces including a 1934-style telephone, which sits on the court bench. A 1934 calendar was sought but could not be found. Pat Kerr, then education specialist at the Truman Library (and wife of the then County Curator Charles Kerr), discovered that the days of 1934 and 1973 fell on the same day of the

week. Taking a 1973 calendar, without any advertising, she altered the date to come up with a perfect answer. They displayed July and August since there were no "Monday holidays" in those months in 1973.

When the Truman Office and Courtroom were re-opened after renovations in 1973, many persons visiting the spaces shared reminiscences. The Rev. Lyndon W. Harper, who during the depression in the 1930s was director of the Civic Relief Commission, recalled the many times he had stood before the Court at the old bench, and presented his expense vouchers to be signed by all three judges. "Many times too," Harper said, "I have set in conference with Judge Truman about relief money matters in his office here."

Charles Kerr recalled a story Mrs. Biter told him about keeping a sack full of quarters in the drawer at her desk. "It seems that many times on matters he considered particularly confidential, Judge Truman sent a messenger rather than to go through the courthouse switchboard. Mrs. Biter said there were always willing runners for quarters in those days."

A black panther sculpture was said to have been given to Truman by a school alumni. When Mrs. Hubert Dowell, heard Kerr's plea for a black panther, she remembered one she had acquired when she was newly married and used as a decorative piece on a mantel. But, she had given it to her oldest  grandson, Steve Dowell. Steve, who was 12-years-old at the time of the 1973 restoration, graciously offered his panther statue for Mr. Truman's desktop.

Another desk in the room is similar to the one used by Judge Purcell, with whom Truman shared the office. The third County Court judge had an office in a room off to the west of the Courtroom (which was repurposed when an elevator shaft was installed in 2013).

A spittoon on the floor was a necessity for making tobacco-chewing visitors comfortable in those days of yesteryear. For whatever reason, it is embossed with "Jackson County."

The most important photo documentation of Truman in this office is an image taken by the *Kansas City Star* on morning of November 10, 1934. Truman, in need of a shave after having likely worked through the night, is seated in his office surrounded by stacks of paperwork. Behind him is a roll-top desk with stacks of papers and framed photographs of his mother, wife and daughter. The panther sculpture sits between the pictures. In front of Truman is a flat desk with county road maps and charts under the glass top.[83]

Jackson County Court courtroom, where Harry S. Truman presided and considered County-related matters at the beginning of the Great Depression.

Today the County Court courtroom features a brass railing originally installed in the 1872 courthouse. Fortunately, it had been safely stored at the Truman Library since the 1967 courtroom renovation.[84]

Only one of the chairs used by the three judges in Truman's days could be found, so the County ordered two other chairs to be built "just like the original."[85]

Ink wells and spectacles like those Truman used were located and installed for exhibit and interpretation.

Round spectacles like those that Truman wore.

One of Truman's responsibilities was to sign each County employee's paycheck.

Original, large, payroll ledgers from the early 1930s are filled with Truman's signatures authenticating each disbursement.

To accomplish the task of signing all those checks, Truman used an autopen duplicating device that was invented and popularized by U.S. President Thomas Jefferson in the early 1800s. Truman would hold one fountain pen in his hand and sign once. The autopen would complete five additional signatures.

**Judge Truman signing checks with an autopen
September 24, 1927.**

The Courtyard Lawn at the County Seat

Settlers to Jackson County began arriving in growing numbers by the mid-1820s. They selected the site of Independence Square as the County Seat for its abundance of fresh springs and its majestic forest of elm, oak, walnut, and hickory. Native-Americans had camped at this location for ages.

The Courthouse courtyard as it appeared on Dedication Day, 1933. Elm trees later suffered from disease and were subsequently replaced in the 1970s.

Even trees planted long ago and that survived urban development have a natural lifespan. And, external forces like drought, sleet, wind, disease, and pests can hasten the demise of these stately treasures.

In the mid- to late-1930s, during the drought of the Great Depression, large elm trees that shaded the bluegrass of the courthouse lawn were removed. The 75+ year-old-trees had been carefully protected during the remodeling and expansion of the courthouse between 1932 and 1933. Unfortunately the drought took two older trees on the south side of the courthouse. Five others were described as being, "scraggly veterans showing clearly the marks of intentional prunings and the scars of seasonal tilts with sleet and wind." A decision was made to replace all 13 elm trees with 18 uniform hard maples.

Urban renewal in the 1970s added lots of earth and a concrete retaining wall around the courthouse. Landscaping that once sloped naturally and gradually away from the building to street level was replaced with a concrete terrace. Trees and landscaping suffered from inadequate water and nutrients, plus the reflective heat from the expansive concrete terrace and surrounding buildings.

Elevation showing concrete walls and steps.

Reversal and return to the pre-urban renewal hardscape allowed for sunny turf in 2013; but, the installation of large shade trees became impractical due to the extensive electrical infrastructure and irrigation system just below the surface.

The grounds surrounding Jackson County Courthouse on Independence Square have long featured selected monuments and statues of interest, including a west-facing equestrian statue of Andrew Jackson, Jackson County's namesake. This statue was presented to Jackson Countians by Harry S. Truman upon his election as President of the United States, and dedicated on December 26, 1949.[86] Originally the equestrian statute was on the east side of the courthouse, and faced east. However, when a Bicentennial statue of Truman was dedicated May 8, 1976, by U.S. President Gerald R. Ford, the Jackson statue was moved to the west side.

Other markers on the courthouse courtyard commemorate Jackson County pioneers; the westward trails that funneled through Independence Square from the 1820s; and, the Civil War battles that raged through the Square in the 1860s. The marker detecting the Square's elevation is discussed separately.

Dedication of an historical marker on the Courthouse grounds, May 1913.

Independence Square and Historic Truman Courthouse Future is Bright

In 2001 the last court using space in the Historic Truman Courthouse relocated to the Eastern Jackson County Courthouse on Kansas Avenue. Through the years other county departments occupied space in the decommissioned courthouse including the Jackson County Parks and Recreation's Heritage Programs, Jackson County Election Board, and nonprofit organizations such as the Community Welfare League, Senior Citizens Craft Shop, and the Jackson County Historical Society.

Over the years many politicians, including several U.S. Presidents, have traveled to this historic landmark to politic, announce public policy, and pay homage to President Truman. At the same time many dedicated and loyal residents have provided leadership though civic involvement and ownership roles in properties surrounding Jackson County's landmark courthouse. One of the Square's best advocates and ambassadors drew inspiration from a past presidential visit.

"On Labor Day 1992, then-Arkansas Governor Bill Clinton chose Independence as the backdrop for his fall U.S. presidency campaign opening. Huddled with about 3,000 people near the Harry S. Truman statue at the Jackson County Courthouse, Cindy and Ken McClain and their five children watched Clinton say that President George H.W. Bush was threatening the middle class that Truman had helped create. That evening, the McClain family scrambled home, anxious to watch the speech on CNN. Instead, they were left with feelings of frustration. *'We were just horrified by how boarded up the Square looked on TV,'* Cindy said, drawing out the syllables of "horrified." *'You don't think about it as much when you're in it, but when you see it from that perspective – they'd pan up every once in awhile to the Secret Service on the roof, and everything was dilapidated.'"*

Jackson County Election Board employees pose with Bill Clinton.

The McClains set out to change the course of Independence Square history that night after Ken turned to Cindy and said, 'This is how I want to spend my income.' "The McClains purchased the former Katz Pharmacy building–boarded up and covered in decades-old campaign signs–and opened Ophelia's Restaurant at 206 N. Main St. in 1998. When Ken, the visionary, walked the building with Cindy, the detail-oriented creative force, they immediately knew a restaurant would be best, *'because people will drive to eat. It just made sense because we knew we had to make this as a destination. We do think about the type of person that needed to come up here in order to save the Square,'* Cindy said."[87]

The seeds sown by the McClains added to efforts of the Independence Square Association, a nonprofit association of merchants, bankers, property owners, and community volunteers who work to revitalize downtown through historic preservation and community participation. They work closely with member businesses, churches, and organizations as a liaison to city, county, and state government entities.

Much transpired between 1995 and the first decade of the new century to make Independence Square a destination once again. Efforts blossomed to restore the historic landmark courthouse that will stand for many more years to come.

The work was divided into three phases between 1995 and 2013.

Historic Courthouse Restoration
Phase I

In April 1995, then Jackson County Executive Katheryn Shields, announced plans to begin refurbishing the courthouse.[88] In 1998, the City of Independence developed a Tourism Strategic Plan that included goals to support revival of the Square and renovation of the courthouse including a master visitors' center. In October 2002, Shields led a tour through the construction after lead paint in the building was removed, electrical upgrades were made, and pigeon droppings had been removed from the attic.[89]Momentum and progress towards a comprehensive renovation plan continued through the decade that included a new slate roof, painting and restoring the clock tower and cupola, brick tuck-pointing and new energy-efficient, historically accurate windows.

Jackson County, the City of Independence and the State of Missouri provided $2 million to complete Phase I of a long-term, three-phase project.[90]

It was discovered that a composition roof had been nailed directly on top of the original 1933 slate roof. All layers had to be removed before a new slate roof could be installed in 2002.

Workers inspect and replace slate roof.

A citizen's task force co-chaired by Chuck Foudree and former Independence Mayor, Barbara Potts, forged ahead with Phase II planning and recommended to the County Executive that removal of tons of Urban Renewal concrete surrounding the courthouse would serve to relieve water pressure on the courthouse foundation. *"Restoring the courtyard to the 1933 design will add sidewalks and nearly 70 parking spaces around the courthouse,"* said Potts.

Historic Courthouse Restoration
Phase II[91]

In December 2008, the 1933-era boilers finally failed and could not be re-started. This event signified the need to initiate Phase II of the courthouse restoration, which was to return the courthouse grounds to their 1933 appearance and address major drainage issues eroding the building's foundation.

On January 30, 2009, Jackson County Executive Mike Sanders announced during a news conference that the condition of Jackson County's Historic Truman Courthouse warranted officially declaring the landmark building a "public emergency."

The public emergency declaration enabled the County, under both the Jackson County Charter and Missouri state statute, to free up money from its state-mandated contingency fund to cover costs in the short-term, of preserving Jackson County's Historic Truman Courthouse.

An estimated $800,000 was needed to complete the crucial Phase II of the restoration. County Executive Sanders pointed out that Phase II was a necessity to prevent the building from deteriorating beyond the point of repair. "Recent engineering reports and further deterioration indicate that we no longer have the luxury of waiting for help to fund the repairs necessary," Sanders said during a news conference, where he was joined by Missouri State Senate Minority Leader Victor Callahan (District 11), State Representative Gary Dusenberg (District 54) and Jackson County Legislator Dennis Waits (3rd District). "If we don't act, we are in danger of effectively losing this historic building." Mr. Sanders thanked Independence Mayor Don Reimal for his partnership. He said the mayor's work on this project has been essential to keeping the restoration effort moving forward.

Urban Renewal retaining walls, concrete terrace, and tons of infill soil aided to the "bathtub effect" described by Mike Sanders.

In 1972, as part of an urban renewal project, retaining walls had been placed around the Historic Truman Courthouse. The very first weekend after those walls were completed, the building suffered its first leak from water seeping into the basement as the walls trapped water around the courthouse. These walls, Sanders said, created a "bathtub effect," sealing water in around the building instead of letting it drain away from it. Removal of those walls, Sanders stressed, was the key component in Phase II as part of saving the building and restoring the courthouse grounds to their 1933 appearance. "Over the last 35 years, with every rain or freeze, this slow water infiltration has quietly been chipping away at the very foundation and

In some locations, the retaining walls were four or five feet tall.

supports that keep the courthouse standing," Sanders indicated.

Phase II began on March 16, 2009, after a contract was awarded to Kidwell Construction Corporation with a bid of $776,005, below the estimated $800,000. The project called for an additional 70 angled parking spaces around the courthouse. "This will bring back a lot of nostalgia to folks who remember when we could park all around the (Independence) Square," said Mayor Reimal.

Parking on the Courthouse side of the Square was lost during Urban Renewal, and restored during Phase II of the construction that began in 2009.

Since bringing down the retaining wall around the Historic Truman Courthouse was an essential step in saving this national landmark, officials from both Jackson County and the City of Independence decided to forego a traditional ground-breaking to commemorate the start of building renovations. Instead, they wielded sledgehammers to help bring down remnants of that wall during a "wall-breaking" ceremony. "The reason so many people are here today is because of the great importance of this courthouse," said Jackson County Executive Mike Sanders. He further stressed, "This is a national, historic building.... Our goal is to once again make this a working courthouse for the people of this community."

Jackson County Executive Mike Sanders addresses spectators for the ground-breaking.

Wielding sledgehammers above, left to right: Ken McClain; Jackson County Parks + Rec Director, Michele Newman; Jackson County Executive, Mike Sanders; Jackson County Public Works Director Jerry Page; and, Independence Mayor, Don Reimal.

At the left: Jackson County Legislator Dennis Waits holds his golden hammer.

Behind the massive walls of Urban Renewal-era concrete is the Harry S. Truman statue, shrouded for protection during the demolition project.

After the ground-breaking ceremony, large, heavy equipment began the process of breaking up tons of Urban Renewal-era concrete around the Courthouse.

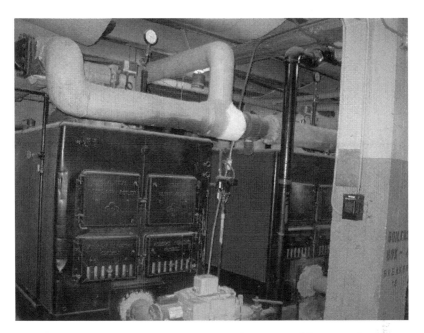

1933 boilers outlived their lifespan. Above shows the system prior to disassembly. Below shows the beginning of the dismantling process.

Each heavy piece had to be hand carried upstairs and out of the building. The remnants (above) and the foundation for a new boiler system (below).

The cast iron sections of the new boiler system (above) took extra large wrenches to tighten together. The completed unit (below) is smaller and much more efficient.

Trees and shrubs that were taken out were mulched for use as erosion control.

Kidwell Construction, the project contractor, took away approximately 4,000 tons of concrete and bricks from the demolition of the courthouse grounds, which were processed as backfill for road beds and other future projects.

Above:
David W. Jackson stands beside an excavated Urban Renewal retaining wall along Lexington Avenue near Liberty, moments before its demolition (as seen at the left).

104

The perimeter of the Courthouse shows the natural elevation after removal of debris and re-grading.

New curbs and sidewalks installed resemble 1933-era infrastructure (above); Sod and Historical markers / monuments were re-installed; a sprinkler system was also added to keep the lawn well-

**Limestone steps leading to the Courthouse
were carefully replaced or restored, as needed.**

On September 3, 2009, it was announced that Phase II renovations were completed on time and under budget. "The weekend after we had the wall taken down this spring, it rained and the basement stayed dry," Sanders said. "With the late snow in March and heavy downpours we've had this summer, I can't imagine how much more damage might have been done to the building's foundation had we not taken the steps we did to get these renovations and repairs done now." Independence Mayor Don Reimal added, *"I may be one of the few here outside of President Truman who can remember coming up here and sitting on this corner and watching the town wind the clock. And now we're rewinding the clock. This is going to be a focal point for Jackson County. The square is going to come back alive...What a day for Jackson County and for Independence. I hope you will make a strong mental note, you were here when this was revitalized. We will continue to make the square and Independence and Jackson County a definite place to be proud of."*

The Harry S. Truman statue remained in its original place throughout the renovations, although the Andrew Jackson equestrian statue had to be temporarily relocated to restore the courthouse lawn. "I think being able to keep the Truman statue in place was symbolic," said Sanders. "It was as if Harry was watching over us the entire project, making sure we got the job done right."

Historic Courthouse Restoration Phase III

While Phases I and II focused on the exterior, Phase III concentrated on the courthouse interior. Renovating the inside of the courthouse was essential to making the facility available for continued use, and transforming it into a working landmark.

Phase III, at estimated cost of $5 million, restored President Harry S. Truman's office and courtroom, addressed critical foundation problems; and brought all interior spaces up to commercial grade under current building codes . . . all while preserving the courthouse's historical integrity.

One large hurdle was to find a suitable location for an elevator to span three floors. Architects repurposed two small spaces on each of the first two floors for the elevator shaft. A deep pit had to be dug in the basement to serve as the footings for the elevator's mechanicals.

Another challenge that architects overcame was allocating suitable spaces for several non-court county departments, as well as the City of Independence Tourism Department and the nonprofit Jackson County Historical Society.

Two small spaces on each of the 1st and 2nd floor were repurposed for the elevator.

Above: Cinderblock foundation to support the new elevator. Below: Ventilation system for heating and cooling utilizes the new boiler.

Outdoor and indoor views of the elevator being installed in its cinderblock shaft.

The courthouse was closed on July 9, 2012, so that renovation work inside the building could begin. This necessitated all tenants to completely vacate the building. By that time, however, the Jackson County Historical Society and Jackson County Public Works were the only two entities needing to pack up and move out. The Society's historically significant collections were sizable. They were temporarily relocated to office and storage spaces on or near the Square.

Archives and Research Library (2011) when located where Assessment is today (2013).

Piper-Wind Architects, Inc., upheld the integrity of the courthouse interior, maintaining its 1933-era look and feel while ingeniously disguising modern conveniences such as heating, ventilation, air conditioning, and technological needs.

Within a year and a half the work was completed by Universal Construction as general contractor, but not before . . .

. . . significant work was performed to further
restore and preserve the clock tower . . . and . . .

. . . major renovations to all interior spaces had to be completed to return as close to possible the 1933-era spaces, while providing for modern conveniences and necessities.

Jackson County Historical Society Archive Center 2nd floor space under renovation.

Jackson County Historical Society Archive Center, in previously unused 2nd floor space at the southeast corner of the Courthouse.

The Jackson County Historical Society operates its History Center (above) and Bookshop (below), in a former vault used by the County.

Across the hall, the City of Independence Tourism
Department offers its Visitors' Experience Center to
welcome visitors and tourists to Independence.

In lower level spaces that were once dilapidated, are now neat, clean, and tidy office spaces for Jackson County's Recorder of Deeds offices.

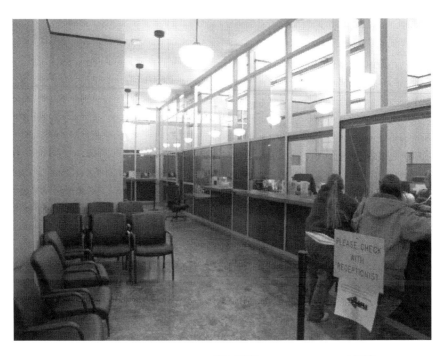

Jackson County's Assessment and Collections Departments enjoy modern offices at the west end of the main, or 1st floor level (above).

Ample storage for the Historical Society's collections is tucked into lower level storage rooms (right).

A Re-Dedication
2013

Jackson County's Historic Truman Courthouse now offers attractions, including tours of President Harry S. Truman's office and the courtroom where he once served as Presiding Judge. Various county departments operate once again in the courthouse. The building now also features an art gallery displaying the Ken and Cindy McClain art collection of George Caleb Bingham masterworks. The Jackson County Historical Society and City of Independence Tourism Department make available a History Center and Experience Center for residents and tourists.

From the Civil War and the Great Depression to Urban Renewal— Jackson County's Courthouse on Independence Square is a survivor. J. Bradley Pace, author of, "Survivors: A Catalog of Missouri's Remaining 19th Century County Courthouses," quoted travel expert Arthur Frommer, who said, *"Tourism does not go to a city that has lost its soul."* Pace added, "The Square—and the Courthouse in particular—are certainly a big part of the soul of Independence and Jackson County."

Harry S. Truman, as Presiding Judge (akin to today's County Executive) of the Jackson County Court (akin to today's County Legislature), presided over the dedication of the newly expanded courthouse on the Square at 2 p.m. on September 7, 1933.

Eighty years later, to the day and time, Jackson County Executive, Mike Sanders, re-dedicated the courthouse on September 7, 2013.

A parade preceded the program, led by the Truman High School Drum Line and followed by Niel M. Johnson, impersonating Harry S. Truman, as he was chauffeured around the Square. The Sons of the American Revolution were also present. The flags were unfurled, the bell in the courthouse clock tower rang at 2 p.m., and Kansas City music great Ida McBeth sang the National Anthem.

Truman High School Drum Line

A parade included Truman High School Drum Line (above); and, Truman re-enactor, Niel M. Johnson (below).

Truman re-enactor Niel M. Johnson

Sons of the American Revolution

The Sons of the American Revolution (above). Sign for the 'new' Historic Truman Courthouse (below).

Color guard presentation (above). Ida McBeth
performing the National Anthem (below).

Ida McBeth performing the national anthem

Clifton Truman Daniel, the president's grandson, greeted everyone to start the festivities and introduced Sanders. Daniel said his grandfather would be pleased with the work done on the restoration. "I think if he was here, he would be more than proud to work here again." Sanders remarked:

Mike Sanders
Jackson County
Executive

"Good afternoon. Thank you for being here today as we mark this momentous occasion.

"I want to thank each of the elected leaders sitting behind me for giving us your time today. Senator Blunt, Congressman Cleaver, and Congressman Skelton -- thank you.

"Mayor Reimal – I want to especially thank you and the City of Independence. The project that we are celebrating this afternoon simply would not have been possible, without your collaboration and cooperation.

"And a special thank you to Jackson County Public Works, Piper-Wind Architects, and Universal Construction for the countless hours you put in to make today a reality.

"Exactly 80 years ago today, on a warm summer afternoon, the citizens of Jackson County gathered in the county seat of Independence to dedicate a newly refurbished and reimagined county courthouse. At that ceremony, then Presiding Judge Harry S. Truman declared:

"Here is your courthouse Jackson County, finished and furnished within the budget set aside to build it."

"Now 80 years later, humbly standing here in Truman's footsteps, as your County Executive, I am proud to once again present the citizens of

Jackson County with your county courthouse, which has been finished on time and on budget.

"The completion of this project is a shining example of how our government can work efficiently and effectively. We can take pride in the fact that this beautiful courthouse behind us is being re-opened to the citizens of Jackson County without asking them for additional tax dollars. To the members of the County Legislature, thank you for your partnership on this project and for making this courthouse a priority of our county government.

"Today's ceremony is the end of a four-year odyssey. Just a few short years ago, it was uncertain how much longer this building would even stand. Decades of damage from storms and rainwater combined with years of neglect put this historic structure at a crossroads. We were told by engineers that without immediate and major repairs to the building's foundation, this courthouse and its rich history could be lost forever.

"In January 2009, the county declared a public emergency so that we could gain access to the funds necessary to save this landmark. The retaining wall that contributed to the weakening of the building's structural integrity was torn down. Parking spaces were added and  improvements were made to the sidewalks and grounds surrounding the courthouse.

"These enhancements were step one in our commitment to restoring the Truman Courthouse to its original glory. The goal was not only to return the building it to its intended design, but to open it back up to the citizens of Jackson County so it could serve its original purpose. The finished project you see behind us meets that stated goal by once

126

again becoming a working courthouse, housing staff from various county departments.

"Additionally, when these courthouse doors open back up in just a few minutes, our citizens will be able to visit the courtroom where President Truman began his political career as well as the historic Brady Courtroom. You will see a museum space filled with world class pieces of art along with a tourism center that welcomes visitors to our community. And as you heard just a few minutes ago -- for the first time in more than 20 years -- the bell on the iconic clock tower is ringing once again and will continue to ring for years to come.

"But today is about more than the building that sits behind us. It marks another key milestone in the revitalization of Independence Square.

"I want to take this opportunity to publicly thank Ken and Cindy McClain. Their passion and commitment towards the revival of the Independence Square has been unwavering. Much of what you see and experience around these few city blocks is due to their vision.

Jackson County's Historic Truman Courthouse was re-dedicated 80 years to the day and time of its last opening in 1933.

127

"During a 1993 speech, Historian and Pulitzer Prize Winning Author David McCullough had this to say about Independence, our county seat.

"History just isn't in books. It's all up and down these streets. And knowing something because it is a fact isn't really knowing something at all. To really know something is when you feel it. And when you come here, you feel the story of Independence, Missouri and thus the story of the United States of America."

"During the Civil War, Union and Confederate troops battled on the ground where we stand today. These same streets were a key meeting point for settlers who were headed west along the Santa Fe, Oregon, and California Trails, in search of a better and more prosperous life. And the key decisions that Truman made as President were based on the ideals he learned while living just a few blocks away on Delaware Street.

"All of us here today are now the stewards of that rich history. It is important that we work to keep the spirit and the memories of this city square alive, not only for our citizens today, but for the generations to come.

"More than anything though, today is a reminder of the man who bears the name of this courthouse....President Harry S. Truman. Shortly after his presidency ended, he returned home. In his typical and endearing no-nonsense style, Truman spoke glowingly of his hometown and our county seat of Independence by saying:

"It's good to be back home, in what I call the center of the world....Independence, Missouri. I think it's the greatest town in the United States and I've been all over the country and I've been to Europe and South America and several other places. But I still like to come back home and I'll continue to feel that way as long as I live. It's the center of things for me and I'm more than happy to be here and to stay here for the rest of my life."

"While President Truman has passed on, his words and his legacy still live on....in this town, in this county, and now, once again....in this Courthouse."[92]

Other speakers present on the re-dedication program included: Independence Mayor Don Reimal; Clifton Truman Daniel, Harry S. Truman's Grandson; former Congressman, Ike Skelton; and, Senator Roy Blunt.

"Take pride in this courthouse," Skelton said. *"Use it and know in the decades ahead that those who follow you will be better off because of the government administrated here."*

Former Senator Ike Skelton

"Reopening the courthouse "will have a real impact not only on Independence's heritage" but also on efforts to revitalize Independence Square," Senator Blunt stated.

Senator Roy Blunt

Sanders, Skelton and Blunt cut the ceremonial ribbon.

JACKSON COUNTY HISTORIC TRUMAN COURTHOUSE

REDEDICATION SEPTEMBER 7, 2013

JACKSON COUNTY EXECUTIVE
MICHAEL D. SANDERS

JACKSON COUNTY LEGISLATURE

Scott Burnett	Dan Tarwater III	Theresa Garza Ruiz
James D. Tindall, Sr.	Gregory Grounds	Crystal Williams
Dennis R. Waits	Bob Spence	Fred Arbanas

Chief Operating Officer	Shelley Temple Kneuvean
Chief of Intergovernmental Relations	Calvin Williford
County Engineer	Earl Newill

Piper-Wind Architects Inc., Architect
Universal Construction Company Inc., General Contractor

Re-Dedicatory plaque installed in the south entrance of the Historic Truman Courthouse.

"Wind the clock" today . . . patronize renovated boutiques and specialty businesses . . . dine at Square restaurants . . . and, enjoy Jackson County's Historic Truman Courthouse.

Check back in 2093 when an 80-year time capsule is scheduled to be opened. It is intended to reveal items Jackson Countians of 2013 thought might have significance or meaning to the future of citizens of Jackson County.

Jackson County Museum of Art

George Caleb Bingham: Witness to History

One extraordinary addition to the renovated Historic Truman Courthouse is the Jackson County Museum of Art, a multi-room gallery solely dedicated to the life and art of George Caleb Bingham (1811-1879), Missouri's famed painter--and 'forgotten' politician.

The exhibit, curated by Patricia Moss, is an opportunity for visitors to view conserved oil portraits and genre prints while glimpsing history through the prism of Bingham's artwork. Moss believes "that art, even more than the written word, reveals a detailed and accurate picture of history." She announced her plans for a "Bingham Portrait Project," in the Autumn 2001 *Jackson County Historical Society JOURNAL.* The Jackson County Museum of Art is one result of those initial thoughts put to paper.

The first "lost" Bingham portrait that Moss studied was a painting in the Society's own collections, that of Judge Thomas Chevis, painted in 1837. Moss notes

Judge Thomas Chevis
Oil on canvas, 1837
Jackson County Historical
Society Collection

in the Winter 2013 *Jackson County Historical Society JOURNAL*, "As a work of art the portrait is exquisite. As history, the back story is that in the last days of the Civil War, Judge Chevis, a Union supporter, was shot in the back for his horse. His story is one of the hundreds of capricious acts of violence at the western border where political affiliation justified personal gain—on both sides."

Bingham home in Independence

Bingham, a Virginia native, grew to adulthood in central Missouri (Boonville and Arrow Rock). In the midst of the Civil War in 1864, he lived in Independence, Missouri, in what is now the Lewis-Bingham-Waggoner Estate, a mansion museum open to the public, near Independence Square.

It was there that Bingham painted perhaps his most famous painting, "Martial Law," or, "Order No. 11." The painting, brushed onto a gingham tablecloth, was so popular that he was able obtain a commission for a second painting. After the war he produced the engraving below, based on the paintings.

"Martial Law / Order No. 11" engraving
Signed by George Caleb Bingham

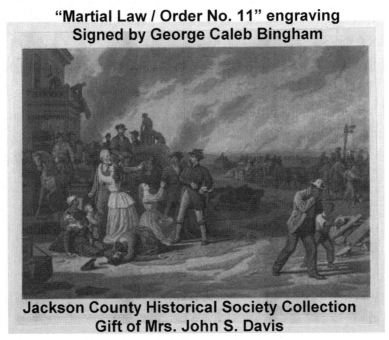

Jackson County Historical Society Collection
Gift of Mrs. John S. Davis

Mary Snell (Mrs. Priestly Haggin) McBride
Oil on Canvas, 1836/1837
McBride's gold, lunar crescent broach was also
passed down in the family, and is also on exhibit.
Kenneth B. and Cynthia McClain Collection

Gallery view and interpretive panels.

An exhibit panel states, "Until recently, most art historians separated Bingham's art from his life." Bingham biographer, Paul Nagel, wrote that *Martial Law*, "might well exemplify the life and nature of George Caleb Bingham. Just as the painting depicts tragedy, sorrow, and conflict, so the career of Bingham was often touched by controversy, pathos, and frustration. His life ranged from moments of high achievement to periods of distress and humiliation. Bingham's powerful paintings may tempt us to imagine that his life was as idyllic as most of the scenes he portrayed, but his surviving papers reveal a far more complicated story."

John Campbell
Oil on Canvas, ca. 1860
His brother's portrait is also on exhibit.
Kenneth B. and Cynthia McClain Collection

Bingham painted for some 40 years. As the exhibit states, "During his lifetime he painted more than 300 portraits, nearly 60 paintings of everyday life, and more than 30 landscapes." One can see his evolution as an artist and how, as Moss describes, "Bingham advanced from the hidden brushstrokes and the brightly lit angular planes typical of American primitivism and luminism to masterful chiaroscuro, undulating curves, rich color and bold impasto." Moss notes, "The exhibition offers a fresh look at the man as a talented, ambitious, persevering frontier artist who modulated cursory training, books of engravings, and a cabinet-making apprenticeship into a distinctive, precisely measured geometric style that informed his lifetime's work."

Authors E. Maurice Bloch, Alberta Wilson Constant, Fern Helen Rusk, Lew Larkin, and Paul Nagel have helped to document Bingham's life. Another underlying message of this exhibition is that the life stories of each of his subjects are worthy of study and publication in and of themselves.

"Artwork for the exhibition primarily came from the collections of Kenneth B. And Cynthia McClain; and also, the State Historical Society of Missouri-Columbia; the personal collection of the art curator, Joan Stack; Jackson County Historical Society; and others," writes Moss.

The Jackson County Museum of Art exhibit, *George Caleb Bingham: Witness to History*, asks viewers, "after reviewing the evidence in the life and art of George Caleb Bingham, what is the 21st century verdict?"

Appendix A

History of the Jackson County Legislature (Previously, the Jackson County Court)

by David W. Jackson

Jackson County's government spans more than 180-years.
This appendix traces the history of Jackson County's government over the last 180+years. The governing body beginning in 1826 was the Jackson County Court, which was superseded by the Jackson County Legislature in 1970.

Listed are the men and women elected or appointed to serve the County. To provide a glimpse of the County's rich past, selected events affecting County history—and the legislative body—are included within this timeline.

Jackson County Court
1826-1971

Prior to the adoption of the current County Charter in 1970, the governing body in Jackson County, Missouri, was called the Jackson County Court, a form of County government that dates back to Jackson County's formation on December 15, 1826.

The County Court, which first convened in spring 1827, consisted of a legislative panel of three individuals popularly elected. Each one's title was "County Judge," which is like a county commissioner common in other areas of the country. Some Missouri counties are still governed by county courts.

Jackson County was divided into two districts for representation purposes with no regard to population. The County Judge for the Western

District represented Jackson County interests in the western part of the County, including Kansas City. The County Judge for the Eastern District represented Jackson County citizens in the eastern half of the County. The third elected position— "Presiding Judge"—led the legislative body and helped as a tie-breaker on difficult decisions when the other two judges were divided and split their votes. This position is similar to the County Executive elected today.

When more than three names are listed in an administration, it means there were vacancies and successors were appointed. The date of succession is provided when known.

1827
Presiding Judge Richard Fristoe
Abraham McClelland
Henry Burrus (August 1829)

1831
Presiding Judge Richard Fristoe
Lewis Jones
Samuel D. Lucas (August 7, 1832)
Richard B. Chiles (February 13, 1833)
John Smith

Washington Irving and friend Charles Joseph Latrobe, spent a few days in Independence in the Autumn of 1832. Irving wrote:

"We arrived at this place [Independence, September 24, 1832] the day before yesterday, after nine days' traveling on horseback from Saint Louis. Our journey has been a very interesting one, leading on across fine prairies and through noble forests, dotted here and there by farms and log-houses, at which we find rough but wholesome and abundant fare and very civil treatment. Many parts of these prairies of Missouri are extremely beautiful, resembling cultivated countries, rather than the savage rudeness of the wilderness.
"Yesterday I was out on a deer hunt in the vicinity of this place, which led me through some scenery that only wanted a

castle, or a gentleman's seat here and there interspersed, to have equaled some of the most celebrated park scenery of England.

"The fertile of all this Western country is truly remarkable. The soil is like that of a garden, and the luxuriance and beauty of the forests exceed any I have seen. We have gradually been advancing, however, toward rougher and rougher life, and are now at a straggling little frontier village that has only been five years in existence. From hence, in the course of a day or two, we take our departure southwardly, and shall soon bid adieu to civilization [the edge of the United States was at State Line until 1854] and encamp at night in our tents. My health is good, though I have been much affected by the change in climate, diet and water since my arrival in the West. Horse exercise, however, always agrees with me. I enjoy my journey exceedingly and look for still greater gratification in the part which is now before me, which will present much greater wildness and novelty. The climax will be our expedition with the Osages to their hunting grounds and the sight of a buffalo hunt."

1834
Presiding Judge Moses G. Wilson
Lawrence Flournoy
Daniel P. Lewis

In 1838, the first, permanent, brick Jackson County Courthouse was erected on Independence Square, the County Seat for Jackson County.

1838
Presiding Judge John Davis
Lawrence Flournoy
John Smith

1842
Presiding Judge James B. Yager
Alvin Brooking
Richard D. Stanley (1844)
Richard Fristoe (1846)
James Smart

1846
Presiding Judge Alvin Brooking
Richard D. Stanley
James Gray (1848)
Walter Bales

A tall, pointed spire was added to the 1838 Jackson County Courthouse in 1846. It was visible for miles around in those days (given that Independence Square is on high ground and at that time few trees obstructed views and vistas).

In April 1846, a 250-wagon train outfitted at mercantile stores and blacksmith shops around Independence Square. The Donner party was among the emigration heading west that spring. As the wagon train traveled westward it began to break up into smaller units. Some emigrants wanted to travel at a different pace; others wanted to take different routes (or cut-offs). The Donner party's fate is a well-documented tragedy.

After gold was discovered in 1848 at one former Jackson Countian's California stake (John Sutter of Westport), a rush for riches ensued. A flood of young men passed through Jackson County on their way to strike it rich in the spring of 1849. The following year, an even larger emigration funneled through our area towards the territory of California (emigrants of 1850 arrived at California's doorstep just as California was admitted to the Union that September).

Mexican War veterans returning from the Southwest in 1848 found the Jackson County Courthouse enlarged, its exterior walls refaced and the building garbed in a form of colonial architecture. It was this courthouse that the multitudes of Oregon and California emigrants would see as they outfitted for their long, arduous journey into the West.

142

1850
Presiding Judge Richard D. Stanley
Walter Bales
Richard Smith

In 1852, Jackson County opened the Jackson County Poor Farm at Little Blue, Missouri. The property was purchased from Cole Younger's father who had extensive land holdings in that area. Though the name of the almshouse changed over the years, the services to the indigent continue today. The site is still owned by the County, and operated and managed under contract by Truman Medical Center, Inc. The Jackson County Courthouse was remodeled in 1853.

1854
Presiding Judge Richard D. Stanley
James Porter
James B. Yager

1858
Presiding Judge Richard D. Stanley
Presiding Judge Nathaniel H. Scruggs (October 1861)[93]
James McClellan
Thomas A. Smart
Robert Weston (October 1861)[94]

1862
Presiding Judge Nathaniel H. Scruggs (October 1862)
        (resigned January 1863)[95]
Presiding Judge Oscar H. Cogswell (appointed January 1863)
        (resigned August 1864)[96]
Jacob Leader
Robert Weston (resigned November 1862)[97]
Lucius Carey (appointed July 1863
        when William O. Shouse failed to qualify)[98]
George W. Toler (commissioned September 1864
        to fill Cogswell's position)[99]

At its November 1863 term, of the Jackson County Court, justices proceeded *"to cast lots for their respective terms as such Justices for 2, 4 & 6 years from the 1ˢᵗ of November 1862, which resulted as follows viz for the 2 year term ending the 1ˢᵗ November 1864, Oscar H. Cogswell; for the 4 year term ending the 1ˢᵗ November 1866, Jacob Leader; for the 6 year term ending the 1ˢᵗ November 1868, Lucius Carey. Ordered that the same be certified by the Secretary of Sate of the State of Missouri."*[100]

The Civil War (1861-1865) in Jackson County was a tumultuous era that wreaked havoc for every individual and family. Even before the other sections of the country knew there was a "War Between the States," Independence and Jackson County were the center of a war-torn territory. The hostilities in our area actually began in 1854, seven years before the outbreak of the war. Lawless raids swept over this territory on the border of slavery. During the war, guerrilla bands from both Missouri and Kansas raided back and forth. The old courthouse looked out on scenes the like of which no other community ever witnessed.

The Battle of Independence and the Battle of Lone Jack, fought respectively on August 11 and August 16, 1862, were parts of the same campaign. They were provoked by leaders who the year before had served under Price in the Missouri State Guard, but they now came with commissions in the Confederate Army on recruiting expeditions.

After the battles citizens without respect to party, flocked to the scenes of strife and did all in their power for the suffering and the dying. The courthouse was used as an emergency ward. Dead bodies were stacked on the lawn.

Administration of government and justice during these years was quite difficult, and in 1863 was surrendered over to the Federal government when martial law was instituted under General Order No. 11. Independence became a Federal post, commanded by Colonel James T. Buell of the 7th Missouri Cavalry, a force of about 500 men, camped partly on the west side of Pleasant Street. Buel's headquarters, with a company or two, was in the old McCoy Bank Building on the Square (southwest corner of current-day Liberty and Lexington). The lot on the corner to the east, later occupied by the Chrisman-Sawyer Bank Building (southeast corner of current-day Liberty and Lexington), was then vacant property.

It was reported that Buel contemplated an attack on the Confederate recruiting camp. This attack was anticipated by Hughes, who at daybreak on Monday morning, August 11, suddenly dashed into Independence and opened fire on Buel's headquarters, from which came a vigorous defensive reply.

Another round of warfare waged through Jackson County in 1864, beginning with the Battle of the Little Blue and followed by the Second Battle of Independence and the Battle of Westport.

Prior to the Civil War, the members of the Jackson County Court were elected to serve four-year terms. As you can see from the dates that followed the War, there was more inconsistency regarding the terms of service on the court.

1865
Presiding Judge Jacob Leader (May 1865)[101]
Minor T. Graham
James D. Allen
Andrew G. Newgent (by June 1866)[102]

1866
Presiding Judge Andrew G. Newgent
Minor T. Graham
Jacob Leader

1867
Presiding Judge G. W. Gates
Lucius Carey
Joshua Petty

1869
Presiding Judge James B. Yager
Lucius Carey
Joshua Petty

1871

Presiding Judge James B. Yager

Lucius Carey

Joshua Petty

The Jackson County Courthouse was remodeled in 1872.

1873

Presiding Judge James B. Yager

Lucius Carey

Luther Mason (May 6, 1873)

A. L. Harris

W. R. Bernard

1875

Presiding Judge Albert Gallatin Williams

James B. Yager

A. M. Allen

T. H. Broughan

Thomas McNamara

During the 10 years immediately following the Civil War, Independence won notoriety as the wildest town in all the West. The pistol ruled. Saloons and gambling houses made for lively nights. The wildest of returning soldiers stalked the streets with ready weapons. The courthouse was the scene where the bust-up of outlaw gangs occurred. The trials of outlaws and their conviction marked the beginning of a day when law ruled again and the legal code took the place of the pistol.

1877

Presiding Judge Josiah Collins

James B. Yager

A. M. Allen

T. H. Broughan

Thomas McNamara (August 1, 1877)

W. E. Hall

1879
Presiding Judge James B. Yager
D. A. Frink
Charles E. Strode

1881
Presiding Judge James B. Yager
William O. Shouse
Charles E. Strode

1883
Presiding Judge Robert L. Adkins
John P. Jones
Frank R. Allen

1885
Presiding Judge Robert L. Adkins
Hugh Lynch
William C. Chiles

1887
Presiding Judge John A. McDonald
Hugh Lynch
William C. Chiles

After 15 years, the Jackson County Courthouse on Independence Square was once again remodeled and enlarged in 1887 under orders of the Jackson County Court.

1889
Presiding Judge John A. McDonald
John N. Smith
Samuel W. Hudson

1891
Presiding Judge Daniel Murphy
Philip J. Honn
Samuel W. Hudson

1893
Presiding Judge Daniel Murphy
Philip J. Honn
James Latimer

1895
Presiding Judge John B. Stone
John N. Smith
James Latimer

1897
Presiding Judge John B. Stone
G. L. Chrisman
J. R. Marsh

1899
Presiding Judge G. L. Chrisman
S. L. Luttrell
E. R. Hunter

1901
Presiding Judge G. L. Chrisman
S. L. Luttrell
John M. Surface

1903
Presiding Judge G. L. Chrisman
Joseph W. Mercer
E. C. O'Rear

1905
Presiding Judge G. L. Chrisman
Joseph W. Mercer
J. M. Patterson

1907
Presiding Judge J. M. Patterson
Charles E. Moss
George J. Todd

The 1907 Jackson County Court decided to call on the general revenue fund again to remodel the courthouse (it had been 20 years since it had last been enlarged), for no bonds up to that point were ever voted for the various changes made to the courthouse. This structure would serve the County Seat for more than 25 years to come.

Also, in July 1908 the cornerstone to the new County Hospital officially dedicated "Patterson Hall," named after Jackson County Court Presiding Judge J.M. Patterson. Within three years, however, "Patterson Hall" was chiseled from the cornerstone at the beginning of 1911. On January 3 the Kansas City Journal reported the following order: "Resolved, by the court, that the county poor farm and hospital buildings known as "Patterson Hall" shall hereafter be known and designated as "The Jackson County Home."[103]

1909
Presiding Judge J. M. Patterson
E. E. Axline
George Holmes

1911
Presiding Judge H. C. Gilbert
E. E. Axline
E. L. Martin

1913
Presiding Judge H. C. Gilbert
R. D. Mize
Theodore Remley

1915
Presiding Judge Miles Bulger
R. D. Mize (died December 19, 1915)
James V. Compton (appointed to fill the vacancy)
Stephen C. Woodson

In 1916 the Jackson County Court helped to preserve the County's first seat of justice, the 1827 Log Courthouse.

1917
Presiding Judge Miles Bulger
S. T. Pendleton
Stephen C. Woodson

Jackson Countians participated in The Great War (which became known as World War I) between 1917 and 1919.

1919
Presiding Judge Miles Bulger
James E. Gilday
George G. Gaugh

In 1920, after a long battle for suffrage, women in the United States gained the right to vote. The first step taken by Jackson County's election board in May 1920 was to add 89 precincts (bringing the total then up to 338 precincts) to permit Kansas City women to cast their first ballot for president (and county and state officials) that November. From statistics obtained from the suffrage states, it was estimated that registration would increase from 60 percent to 80 percent with women voting. While registration at that time was 79,000, it was estimated that the Kansas City women vote was 50,000 strong.

The women of Jackson County demonstrated their desire to take a hand in the conduct of the affairs of government by exercising their right of suffrage in the first day of registration (September 28) in the "country precincts" outside Kansas City. Turnout far outweighed expectations, and it was estimated that the total number of voters would triple the 1916 turnout. The Jackson County League of Women Voters on October 31, 1920, urged all women who voted to display an American flag at the front of their home on that day in recognition of the right that was recently granted.

1921
Presiding Judge Miles Bulger
James E. Gilday
George E. Kimball

1923
Presiding Judge Elihu W. Haycs
Harry S. Truman
Henry F. McElroy

1925
Presiding Judge Elihu W. Hayes
H. W. Rummell[104]
Daniel G. Stewart

1927
Presiding Judge Harry S. Truman
Robert W. Barr
Howard J. Vrooman

During World War I, Truman had become friendly with Jim Pendergast. In mid-1921 when Truman and Jacobson's haberdashery was flourishing, Jim's father, Mike, asked Truman if he would like to run for judge of the county court for the eastern district. His offer was declined, but Truman eventually entered into the race as an independent.

Jackson Countians then—as now—owe Truman much gratitude for his vision and successful execution of a multitude of decisions that kept Jackson County at the forefront of forward-thinking county planning, civic up-building, good government, welfare and healthcare issues. County Court minutes are full of details that tell the story of how Jackson County survived (and in some instances thrived) during the Great Depression of the 1930s.

1929
Presiding Judge Harry S. Truman
Robert W. Barr
Thomas B. Bash

1931
Presiding Judge Harry S. Truman
E. I. Purcell
W. O. Beeman

1933
Presiding Judge Harry S. Truman
E. I. Purcell
Battle McCardle

Under Harry S. Truman as Presiding Judge, Jackson County voters passed a multi-million dollar bond issue. This measure was instituted at the onset of the Great Depression. It helped pump money into the local economy for works projects like building bridges, roads and civic structures. The Jackson County Courthouse in downtown Kansas City, Missouri, was constructed from this bond measure. And, the Jackson County Courthouse at the County Seat on Independence Square was remodeled.

1935
Presiding Judge Eugene I. Purcell
J. W. Hostetter
Battle McCardle

1937
Presiding Judge David E. Long
J. W. Hostetter
Battle McCardle

1939
Presiding Judge David E. Long
F. L. Byam
Fred W. Klaber

1941
Presiding Judge George S. Montgomery
Leslie I. George
Fred W. Klaber

1943
Presiding Judge George S. Montgomery
Walter L. Yost
Fred W. Klaber

1945
Presiding Judge George S. Montgomery
Walter L. Yost
Fred W. Klaber

By serving in World War II, Jackson Countians stood bravely in the effort to combat the Axis powers that were terrorizing Europe, Asia and the Pacific.

1947
Presiding Judge Harry M. Gambrel
William J. Randall
Fred W. Klaber

1949
Presiding Judge Harry M. Gambrel
William J. Randall
Fred W. Klaber

1951
Presiding Judge Harry M. Fleming
William J. Randall
Fred W. Klaber

1953
Presiding Judge Harry M. Fleming
William J. Randall
Henry H. Fox Jr.

1955
Presiding Judge Ray G. Cowan
William J. Randall
Hunter Phillips

1957
Presiding Judge Ray G. Cowan
William J. Randall
Hunter Phillips

1959
Presiding Judge John J. Kopp
William J. Randall (Floyd L. Snyder Sr., March 6)
Hunter Phillips

1961
Presiding Judge John J. Kopp
Floyd L. Snyder, Sr.
Hunter Phillips

1963
Presiding Judge Charles E. Curry
Floyd L. Snyder Sr.
Hunter Phillips

1965
Presiding Judge Charles E. Curry
Floyd L. Snyder Sr.
Morris Dubiner

1967
Presiding Judge Charles E. Curry
Alex M. Petrovic
Charles B. Wheeler

1969
Presiding Judge Charles E. Curry
Alex M. Petrovic
Charles B. Wheeler

1971-1972
Presiding Judge George W. Lehr
Joe Bolger, Jr.
Harry Wiggins

One of the major accomplishments of the County Court at this time was the successful passage, planning and construction of the Truman Sports Complex. The noncurrent, historical records of the Jackson County Sports Authority are preserved in the Jackson County Historical Society's Archives. Alex M. Petrovic, Charles B. Wheeler, Harry Wiggins and Floyd L. Snyder Sr., have also donated some of their personal papers to the Society's collections.

Jackson County Legislature
Since 1973

Jackson County voters adopted the current Charter in 1970, creating a new form of government featuring administrative departments headed by appointed personnel under an elected Legislature, with one elected County Executive. These are the individuals elected to serve as legislators or the County Executive since the first elections under the current Charter were held in November of 1972. Appointments to fill vacancies are included in parentheses.

January 1973 - December 1974
County Executive - George W. Lehr
1st District at Large - Ted Newman
2nd District at Large - Lee Vertis Swinton
3rd District at Large - Dr. Harry Jonas
4th District at Large - Fred Arbanas
1st District - I. Pat Rios
2nd District - Ronald C. Spradley
3rd District - Mike White
4th District - Mamie F. Hughes
5th District - Harold (Doc) Holliday Jr.
6th District - Beverly P. Parks
7th District - Virgil Troutwine
8th District - James M. Taylor
9th District - Don C. Redding
10th District - Everett Carlson
11th District - Joe Bolger Jr.

These individuals were elected in November of 1972 to serve two-year terms as part of the transition to the new form of government. Starting in November of 1974, legislators and the County Executive have been elected to four-year terms.

January 1975 - December 1978
County Executive - Mike White
1st District at Large- Ted Newman
2nd District at Large - Lee Vertis Swinton
3rd District at Large - Archie McGee
4th District at Large - Fred Arbanas
1st District - I. Pat Rios
2nd District - Ronald C. Spradley
3rd District - Kay Waldo
4th District - Mamie F. Hughes
5th District - Harold (Doc) Holliday Jr.
6th District - Beverly P. Parks / Rev. John Giacopelli[105]
7th District - Virgil Troutwine
8th District - Robert V. Jacobi
9th District - Harry Griffitts
10th District - Bob Johnson
11th District - Joe Bolger, Jr.

January 1979 - December 1982
County Executive - Dale Baumgardner
1st District at Large - Albert Riederer / David L. Young[106]
2nd District at Large - J. W. Patterson
3rd District at Large - Archie McGee
4th District at Large - Fred Arbanas
1st District - Frank D. Palermo
2nd District - Charlotte Musgrave / Ed Growney[107]
3rd District - Douglas A. Young, Jr.
4th District - Pat Cowan-Scaggs
5th District - Harold (Doc) Holliday Jr.
6th District – William F. Waris
7th District - Virgil Troutwine
8th District - Robert Beaird
9th District - Edith Selders / Richard F. Schmidt[108]
10th District - Robert Thane Johnson / Dr. Robert E. Hertzog[109]
11th District - Joe Bolger Jr.

January 1983 - December 1986
County Executive - William F. Waris
1st District at Large - David L. Young
2nd District at Large - J. W. Patterson
3rd District at Large - Archie McGee
4th District at Large - Fred Arbanas
1st District - Frank D. Palermo / Henry Rizzo[110]
          Roger Cunningham[111]
2nd District - Fred J. Sanchez
3rd District - Ed Growney
4th District - James D. Tindall, Sr.
5th District - Harold (Doc) Holliday Jr. / Carol Coe[112]
6th District - John E. Redmond
7th District - Robert Watson
8th District - Robert Beaird
9th District - Richard F. Schmidt
10th District - Dr. Robert E. Hertzog / Cecil A. Vaughan[113]
11th District - Bill Randall Williams

During this administration, the number of legislative districts was reduced from 11 to six.

January 1987 - December 1990
County Executive - William F. Waris
1st District at Large - John Carnes / Silvia Rizzo[114]
2nd District at Large - Carol Coe
3rd District at Large - Fred Arbanas
1st District - Roger Cunningham
2nd District - James D. Tindall, Sr.
3rd District - Dennis Waits
4th District - Ed Growney
5th District - Robert Beaird / Mary Lou Smith[115]
6th District - Dr. Robert E. Hertzog

January 1991 - December 1994
County Executive - Marsha Murphy
1st District at Large - Silvia Rizzo
2nd District at Large - Claire McCaskill / Lisa White Hardwick[116]
3rd District at Large - Fred Arbanas
1st District - Dominick Armato / John Patrick Burnett[117]
2nd District - James D. Tindall, Sr.
3rd District - Dennis Waits
4th District - Ed Growney
5th District - Mary Lou Smith
6th District - Dr. Robert E. Hertzog

January 1995 - December 1998
County Executive - Katheryn Shields
1st District at Large - Victor E. Callahan
2nd District at Large - Lisa White Hardwick
3rd District at Large - Fred Arbanas
1st District - John Patrick Burnett
2nd District - James D. Tindall, Sr. / Carl W. Bussey[118]
3rd District - Dennis Waits
4th District - Dan Tarwater, III
5th District - Dixie M. Flynn
6th District - John C. Graham, Sr.

January 1999 - December 2003
County Executive - Katheryn Shields
1st District at Large - Victor E. Callahan
2nd District at Large - Lisa White Hardwick / Bill Petrie[119]
3rd District at Large - Fred Arbanas
1st District - Scott Burnett
2nd District - Ronald E. Finley
3rd District - Dennis Waits
4th District - Dan Tarwater, III
5th District - Terry Young
6th District - Bob Spence

In 2001, Jackson County's 175th Anniversary was celebrated. Several activities and programs were developed and promoted as part of this landmark event recognizing triumphs over challenges.

January 2003 - December 2006
County Executive - Katheryn Shields
1st District at Large - Robert A. Stringfield
2nd District at Large - Bill Petrie / Henry C. Rizzo[120]
3rd District at Large - Fred Arbanas
1st District - Scott Burnett
2nd District - Ronald E. Finley / Eugene Standifer, Jr.[121]
3rd District - Dennis Waits
4th District - Dan Tarwater, III
5th District - Rhonda L. Shoemaker
6th District - Bob Spence

Extensive preservation measures to restore the 1933 Jackson County Courthouse in Independence, and the 1934 Jackson County Courthouse in Kansas City began during this administration.

January 2007-December 2010
County Executive - Mike Sanders
1st District at Large - Theresa Garza Ruiz
2nd District at Large - Henry Rizzo
3rd District at Large - Fred Arbanas
1st District - Scott Burnett
2nd District - James Tindall, Sr.
3rd District - Dennis Waits
4th District - Dan Tarwater, III
5th District – Greg Grounds
6th District - Bob Spence

The renovation and expansion of the Truman Sports Complex was one Jackson County project commenced during this administration.

Additionally, the two properties owned by Jackson County and leased by Truman Medical Center Corporation (TMC) enjoyed expansion and remodeling programs for the benefit of citizens. The County's dedication to caring for its indigent is a tradition of compassion that dates back to at least 1852, when this site was first acquired (today TMC-Lakewood).

January 2011-December 2014
County Executive - Mike Sanders
1st District at Large - Theresa Garza Ruiz
2nd District at Large – Crystal Williams
3rd District at Large - Fred Arbanas
1st District - Scott Burnett
2nd District - James D. Tindall, Sr.
3rd District - Dennis Waits
4th District - Dan Tarwater, III
5th District - Greg Grounds
6th District - Bob Spence

Renovations to Jackson County's Historic Truman Courthouse continued during this term. The historic structure was re-dedicated on September 7, 2013. Work also commenced to remodel the Eastern Jackson County Courthouse at 308 West Kansas, in Independence, for spaces dedicated to Jackson County's court system.

Jackson County Legislature, 2011-2014

Appendix B

A Guided Tour of Architecture on the Historic Independence Square

The following tour guides visitors around historic Independence Courthouse Square. It encompasses the immediate first-block, or nucleus of downtown Independence, Missouri.

It is hoped that adjacent property owners extending to the blocks beyond the Independence Square may be inspired to share their compiled history for preservation in the Jackson County Historical Society's Archives. Contributed data about individual buildings might also be included in future editions of this publication. Patrick H. Steele, Sr., former Historic Preservation Manager for the City of Independence, conducted considerable research to develop the material presented below. This extract is published with his permission.

A commercial loan program sponsored by the City of Independence Community Development Block Grant Program and State and Federal Historic Preservation Tax Credits has aided property owners in adaptively reusing their older, historic buildings.

In the 15 years since the following information was first compiled, the Square has and continues to experience positive transformations. While some buildings continue to carry an historical name, recent and/or current (2013) businesses and supportive data has been added [in brackets] by author, David W. Jackson, for timeliness and clarity.

Originally prepared by Patrick H. Steele, Sr.
for National Historic Preservation Week,
May 8-15, 1999, sponsored by the
Independence Heritage Commission

From the time of its platting as the seat of Jackson County in 1827, through the Santa Fe Trail days, the Civil War, and the Truman era; the Independence Courthouse Square has witnessed some of the most monumental events, both in the history of Independence, and in the history of America's expansion west. Serving as a reminder of this rich heritage, the Square is fortunate to have retained a significant collection of 19th and 20th century architecture. But, with such a diverse display of building designs and remodeling, the historic significance of this architecture cannot always be easily deciphered, at least not by the average person. To understand the history and development of architecture on the Independence Square we must first have an understanding of the pattern of commercial development in America as a whole—a pattern that began at the time of settlement, and that has continued to evolve, even up through current efforts geared towards downtown revitalization.

Historically, America's success has been closely related to the settlement of its territory and the growth of its population. Town building was the primary focus of westward expansion during the 19th century and many Americans shared the dream that their own communities would one day emerge as great urban centers. Because private venture was key to the nations' development, commercial architecture came to play a major role in defining the character of its settlements.

The size and distinction of a community's commercial buildings reflected both its achievements and its potential. In frontier towns like Independence, many of the earliest and finest permanent buildings were erected to house commercial and institutional enterprises. Businesses were intentionally clustered in a central district that would serve as the hub for town activities. In Independence, the development of the public square and its commercial center was probably largely determined by the 1827 platting of the Jackson County seat.

The individuality of the stores, offices, banks and hotels that made up a commercial district were just as important as their collective personality; after all, a building's storefront served not only as an advertisement for their business within, but also as a direct reflection of the proprietor's expertise. Technology and the mass production of building materials, including elaborate trim and glass window treatments, allowed buildings to take on a distinctive appearance of their own and architectural style became a tool for stimulating rivalry in the marketplace.

Accordingly, storefronts have always been directly associated with myths about progress and change, and especially about the need to change appearance in order to stay competitive. The history of America's commercial architecture has become a history of remodeling, and the architecture on the historic Independence Square offers no exception to that rule.[122]

Tour Stop No. 1:
Jackson County's Historic Truman Courthouse [1933]
112 West Lexington Avenue

Jackson County's Historic Truman Courthouse, although not a commercial building, has had its own history of remodeling that was inspired by the desire to faithfully reaffirm Independence's significance as the seat of Jackson County....

Undoubtedly selected for its monumental qualities, as with many public and institutional buildings after the turn-of-the-century, the neo-Georgian style is represented here by:

A The 6 over 9 window sash glazing patter and the rounded arches laid in the brick pattern above the first floor windows;
B The accentuated doorways with decorative, triangular pediments over-top that are supported by slender classical columns;
C Quoins (pronounced "coins"), or the rectangular limestone blocks used to accentuate corners;
D A roof-line balustrade, or railing, composed of limestone balusters;
E The similar treatment of the clock-tower, or cupola (pronounced "ku-po-la"); and, the symmetrical arrangement of window and door openings.

165

Tour Stop No. 2:
The Emporium Building [1951]
111 North Main

On the southeast corner of Main Street and Maple Avenue once stood the Ott & Mitchell Furniture and Undertaking establishment, which was founded ca. 1875 by Christian Ott.

The original building was an impressive three-story, brick structure constructed in the Italianate style. Italianate commercial architecture is easily identified by its elaborate treatment of the cornice, or the ornamental moulding that protrudes along the top of the building and is often made of cast iron or pressed tin. Windows are also accentuated with elaborate crown mouldings and are long and narrow with one or two panes of glass in each sash. Of all the commercial storefronts built in America before 1900, the Italianate storefront made of cast iron or of iron and brick was a prevailing model. Historically, this practice held true for Independence Square.

This property was formerly the location of Sampson's, a men's furnishings store, which was founded in 1849 by Moses Sampson. At the time of its closing in 1929, Sampson's was believed to have been the oldest business in Jackson County to continually operate under the same name. [A ledger of Sampson's is preserved in the Jackson County (Mo.) Historical Society Archives.]

The Ott building was destroyed by fire in 1950 and the remains of the building were demolished to make way for the expansion of Kresge (pronounced "kresky") Company, which was located next door. S. S. Kresge Company was a five-and-dime store established in 1929 at 111 North Main Street.

The two-story building was razed by Kresge's to make way for a modern, fireproof store that resembled in style the newly constructed Bundschu Building next door. Kresge's store took on the simpler, more restrained appearance that was common during the  post-World War II period. A modern glass store front and corner entry were added, enhancing the display of merchandise. A polished, stone tile was applied above on the main level to serve as the backdrop for the modern "S. S. Kresge Co." sign.

Tour Stop No. 3:
Bundschu Building [1928]
103 North Main Street

The A. J. Bundschu Building was formerly the site of Independence's first theater, the Wilson Opera House. The Opera House was a grand Italianate theater that was constructed around 1873 by brothers Samuel, Charles, and Rufus Wilson. It was a two-story, high-ceiling building that housed a grocery store on the first floor and an opera house and ball room that seated nearly 600 people on the second floor. In 1883, the Bundschu store was established here, and A. J. Bundschu continued to operate his store in the converted theater for nearly 40 years. Bundschu subsequently purchased the structured on either side of the Opera House, which both dated back to the pre-Civil War period.

In 1928, the three Bundschu properties were demolished to make way for a modern, three-story department store designed by Alonzo H. Gentry. On the evening of March 13, 1928, 500 Independence residents gathered to celebrate the past glory of the Wilson Opera House. Men and

women came dressed in the style of the 1870s. Newspaper accounts reported that, "The ladies wore the becoming gowns of the early period and the men were typical dandies, all so youthful in their appearance and actions that they were accused of slyly holding hands as the stage performance progressed." The entire event was broadcast over KMBC radio. The next day, the work to raze the old structure began.

The new store was the first, modern fireproof commercial building to be erected in Independence, and the first building to have an elevator.

The style of the building reflects some influence from the early Art Deco period, which was characterized, in part, by an emphasis on verticality created through the use of rectilinear forms that are spread at regular intervals and extend the full height of the façade. As with the Bundschu building, smaller piers capped with stylized geometric motifs were often used to further divide the vertical rhythm of the design. The decorative floral reliefs just above the window openings are made of glazed terra cotta and are not characteristic of the Art Deco style. The storefront originally had a series of department store windows on the ground floor, which were enclosed in the 1970s when the building housed City of Independence offices. The Bundschu family sold the store to Emery, Bird, Thayer and Company, in 1959, who continued to operate the store under the Bundschu name until it closed in 1968.

Tour Stop No. 4:
Farmers and Merchants Bank Building [1925]
101 North Main

In 1925, the building on the northeast Corner of North Main Street and East Lexington Avenue housed the Farmers and Merchants Bank, and was the meeting site of the well-known Harpie Club. The Harpie Club was a social organization supposedly interested only in card playing and socializing. However, history tells us that this group probably played an important role in the furthering of Harry S. Truman's political career. The Club was made up of Truman's friends who were mostly former World War I veterans and included many Jackson County employees.... The President was also known to work in a game or two with the old group during his return trips home. [In the late 1950s, Truman was presented with a cocktail bar fashioned in the shape of a "T," and it may well likely have been used in the Harpie Club. It is on display by the Jackson County Historical Society in its museum, the 1859 Jail and Marshal's Home.]

While this building does not reflect a distinct style of architecture, it does tell us about a type of commercial building composition that was

prevalent in the U.S. from the 1850s to the 1950s—the two-part commercial block. The two-part block is characterized by a horizontal division into two distinct zones, which suggests the difference in use on the inside. The treatment of the lower zone with display windows and main entry, clearly indicates its intended use as a public space; while the treatment of the upper portion indicates a private use such as offices, hotel rooms, or in this case, a meeting hall for the members of the Harpie Club.

[To give a sense of evolution of structures on Independence Square, Jackson County (Mo.) Historical Society members Suzee Oberg and Larry Soldanels contributed a deed pertaining to one of their ancestors from July 1860: *"Whereas P. O'Connell being the owner of Lot Number 53 of the Old Town Independence, Missouri, conveyed the same by deed of Trust to Hovey and Henry...and Whereas John Soldan-Ells owning the lot next south and adjoining is about to erect a brick building on it. Now will agree that said Soldan-Ells north wall shall be placed on the line half and half and that whoever shall hereafter build on the O'Connell Lot may put his joists into said wall as a party wall and shall pay one half of the actual cost of said wall whenever said party wall shall be used to build to on the O'Connell Lot."*[123]

The O'Connell Lot is what is believed to have become the Wilson Opera House described in the previous tour stop above.

Today (2013), the building is occupied by a specialty boutique called, Design Living.]

[This intersection is the dividing point for all streets in Independence. Addresses with a "North" designation, will be north of Lexington Avenue; similarly, streets with a "South" designation, will be south of Lexington Avenue.

If you are seeking an address with an "East" directional, it will be east of Main Street; similarly, "West" directionals will be west of Main Street.]

171

Tour Stop No. 5:
Wilson Brother's Block / Carl Building [1887/1912/1950s/1970s]
101-103 ½ South Main Street

Constructed in 1887, the Wilson Brother's Block at the southeast corner of South Main Street and East Lexington Avenue was once considered a model of architectural beauty by the citizens of Independence. Italianate in design, this two-story masonry structure was actually constructed as two separate buildings. At the time of their construction, both buildings once displayed elaborate pressed metal cornices with ornamental brackets in the eave, or that portion of the roof that projects out away from the building. And, the building a 103 ½ was capped with an imposing, decorative pediment. Both buildings have since been substantially remodeled. Just after the turn-of-the-century, around 1906, Ferdinand Carl purchased the corner property from R. D. Mize, who had established a drug store in the original building when it was constructed. Mr. Carl, whose name is still visible on the store name block inset in the center of the parapet wall, must have supervised this major renovation at the time of purchase.

By 1912, the entire storefront had been reworked using a castellated (pronounced "castle-lated") parapet wall, trimmed in cut stone,

and a modern plate-glass storefront with corner entry. Quoins, or the rectangular cut-stone blocks similar to those on the courthouse, were also added to accentuate the corners of the building. This projecting window on the north side represents an

172

addition made sometime before 1950 when the store was occupied by Milgram grocery store. The rear of the building is part of the original structure, as evidenced by the dentiled frieze, or decorative brick band, located just below the roof line and the segmented brick arches over the two narrow windows.

The storefront at 103 ½ South Main Street (the south half of the current office supply store) was also re-worked by 1912, removing the shaped metal parapet and elaborate door surround from 1887. A simpler brick parapet wall was constructed using cut stone trim, taking on an appearance in keeping with its newly remodeled neighbor. The row of dentils, or small teeth-like squares, and the recessed square pattern just below the cornice line, were part of this early remodeling. The only remaining element of the original Italianate storefront is the arcade of windows on the second floor. Sometime before 1950, the entire second story of this facade was sheathed in a layer of stucco, a building material that gained popularity after 1920. The modern plate glass storefront, polished stone sheeting, and ceramic time on the ground level were applied by Montgomery Ward, owners in the early 1970s.

[Jackson County's largest slave owner, Jabez Smith, sold an 81' x 41' corner of Lot 60 to brothers, John and Joseph Soldan-Ells, in July 1857.[124] Documentation has not yet surfaced supporting the "Carl" Building, as identified by a 'cornerstone' of sorts above the main entrance. Today (2013), Alliance Office Products occupies this building which had long been Desktop Office Supply Company.]

Tour Stop No. 6:
Smith-Bormaster Shoe Store Building [1951]
101 West Lexington Avenue
Western Army Store Building [early 1900s/1957]
103 West Lexington Avenue

Since the 1950s, the south side of the Square has experienced major changes. The east end once had an important 19th century, two-story building that was destroyed by fire between 1950 and 1951. [The Smith Shoe and Barber Shop was there in the 1950 Independence city directory; by 1952, the Bormaster Shoe Store occupied the space. Since 1974, it has been part of the Western Army Store duplex, which has also occupied an early 1900s building at 103 West Lexington Avenue since 1957.]

Technological advances in building materials affected the appearance of commercial architecture during the early- to mid-20th century. Usually applied directly over existing historic materials, a veneer of corrugated metal, stucco, porcelain tile, or pigmented glass known as Carrara (pronounced "Ca-rar-a") Glass or Vitrolite had the ability to create the look of a new and up-to-date building. For many buildings, these materials were used to create the slick, shiny surfaces and streamlined appearances that were characteristic of later trends in the Art Deco and Art Moderne periods...

174

Interestingly, while most major cities in the country celebrated the Art Deco and Moderene periods during the 1930s and 1940s, Independence did not really jump on the band wagon until after 1950. While no pure examples of this period in architecture are represented on Independence Square, remnants can still be seen scattered here and there.

Tour Stop No. 7:
Puckett Fruit Company Building [early 1900s/1951]
105 West Lexington Avenue
Café Building [ca. 1925]
107 West Lexington Avenue]

For example, the shiny, black porcelain sheeting that was applied around 1951 to the 19th century brick face of the Puckett Fruit Company Building at 105 West Lexington Avenue, is still intact, as is the thin layer of stucco atop. [This building is vacant as of 2013; Puckett Fruit Company is the earliest tenant so far found to have occupied this building.]

The building at 107 West Lexington Avenue once had a fine Spanish Mission style shaped parapet that probably dated to around 1925. [It was a restaurant/café/buffet under many names since the 1920s, hence its name as the Café Building; as of 2013, the Game Café are occupants.]

Tour Stop No. 8:
109 West Lexington Avenue [1970s]
111 West Lexington Avenue [Peiser Building; demolished]

The building at 109 West Lexington Avenue is a product of a period in American architectural history commonly referred to as Urban Renewal, when policies of clearance and redevelopment were the primary focus for many declining commercial centers. Forced to compete with the new suburban shopping centers that became easily accessible with the growth of the automobile industry and new interstate highway systems, cities struggled to draw folks back downtown through new remodeling efforts that incorporated modern suburban qualities.

[As of 2013, Primary Colors Gallery occupies this building.]

When the three-story, 19th century brick Peiser Building next door to the west at 111 West Lexington was destroyed by fire in the early 1970s, the void provided for more parking space, which was being identified by proponents of Urban Renewal in Independence as a primary need in order to insure successful revitalization of the Square. [Today (2013), the vacancy has been adaptively reused as a garden terrace courtyard for diner's patronizing the Courthouse Exchange restaurant.]

This building formerly at 111 West Lexington was destroyed by fire and was never re-built. It served as a small parking lot until 2002 when it was adaptively re-used as a restaurant courtyard (above),

Tour Stop N. 9:
Martin Building [ca. 1908]
113-115 West Lexington Avenue

This site was formerly the location of the Joseph Mercer Building, a three-story, brick structure constructed around 1888. On February 4, 1906, the building burned in an apparent electrical fire, the first of four fires that took place on Independence Square this same year. First word of the fire came at 12:10 a.m., and by the time the fire department arrived the building was being described as, "a roaring furnace." The newspaper reported that, luckily, two fire walls put into the building's structure protected the adjoining buildings from damage. In all, there was over $70,000 in damages to the building and its contents. Mr. Mercer had announced the rebuilding of his burned structure. However, these plans were prevented by his sudden death on March 16. The property was purchased by Jesse L. Martin in 1908, whose name is associated with the current structure, known as the Martin Building.

The Martin Building's design was originally simple and restrained in style, a popular trend just after the turn-of-the-century when commercial architecture was being viewed as a mechanism for conveying a sense of order and balance. This new approach was based on the idea

Martin Building, as it appeared around 1910.

that while each façade should have its own identity, the overall effect should not reflect the harsh competition of the marketplace.

Additionally, while the design of a building's face would be influenced by the unity and order that is characteristic of the Classical tradition, there should be little,

if any, reference to past architectural styles. On the Martin Building, only simple keystones, or the carved stones placed in the center above each window opening, and a thin stone belt course above were used for adornment. The yellow glass tiles applied on the street level were a later alteration made in the 1950s.

As a side note, the Courthouse Exchange Restaurant, which currently occupies the basement of this building [that was formerly J. C. Penney & Company department store and lunchroom], has a long history in Independence. In 1895, Joseph Poggenpohl, Sr., who came to American from Westphalia, Germany, purchased a business at 116 West Maple

Avenue, to establish a saloon, which he called the Courthouse Exchange. He and his son, Joseph Jr., operated the saloon until 1908 when the business was sold to E. I. Purcell. Subsequently, Purcell became Eastern District Judge of the Jackson County Court.

Tour Stop No. 10:
Elliott Theater Building [1924]
119 West Lexington Avenue

In April 1921, Solon Toothaker purchased a 99-year lease on this property, promising to build a $100,000 motion picture theater that would provide high class vaudeville entertainment. The existing Ott Building, a three-story, late 19th century brick commercial structure that had been damaged by fire, was demolished to house the new operation. William S. McCoy, architect and former Mayor of Independence, Missouri, was hired as the supervising architect and was assisted by Carl Boller, a nationally known theater architect from Kansas City.

Known as the Elliott Theater Building, the present building was erected in 1924.

It, too, displays the same Classical sense of order and unity that influenced its neighbor through the use of modest cut stone pilasters, or the shallow rectangular columns that are mounted to the wall surface, a stone belt course, and patterned brickwork. Continuing a 19th century practice in theater design, this building still incorporated the practicality of usable office or retail space above. Unlike earlier entertainment establishments from the 19th century, the presence of a theater became much more conspicuous in early 20th century architecture. Features that would distinguish the building were added, including large comfortable

 lobbies and elaborate marquees similar to one that once graced this building. The building has since been updated for retail use, using massive plate glass windows and modern, polished tile.

[As of 2013, this building is vacant. It was DuVall's for many years; and, the most recent, long-time location of Gary Plowman's Studio III photographic studio.]

Tour Stop No. 11:
Owens-Wyatt Building [ca. 1895]
121-123 West Lexington Avenue

This example of 19th century commercial building is distinguished by a double-wide brick front with multiple entries. Constructed around 1895 as the Owens-Wyatt Building, it was originally designed to house two storerooms at the street level, with two apartment units above accessed from a center staircase. The second floor may still be used as private office space.

The architectural style has been identified as late Italianate, characterized a bracketed, pressed metal cornice and two stylized pediments, which have been removed in later remodeling. A rich textural effect on the second floor has been created through the use of terra cotta panels, and represents one of the finest displays of terra cotta treatment on a commercial building in Independence. A structural support beam

between the first and second floor of the building has been disguised by the application of small, floral jewels, a technique often used in late 19th century commercial building design. The existing plate glass windows are a remodeling in place before 1950, and the original window transoms above have been covered with modern materials.

[As of 2013, Music Gear occupies 121 West Lexington Avenue, and Craig Jones Taxidermy is located at 123 West Lexington Avenue.]

Tour Stop No. 12:
First National Bank Building [originally ca. 1930; remodeled ca. 1970]
129 West Lexington Avenue

The built history of the three corners at Lexington and Liberty Avenues have been largely impacted by trends in modern commercial architecture, remodeling, and Urban Renewal.

Regarding the bank building on the southeast corner, 129 West Lexington Avenue, who would believe that under these massive walls of porous, white stucco panels and tinted glass still exists the shell of a magnificent ca. 1930 Art Deco building? And, even before that stood a grand, three-story model of 19th century Italianate architecture that had been constructed in 1874.

Historically known as the First Nations Bank, and one of three banking institutions established on corners of the Courthouse Square prior to the turn-of-the-century, this property has been pivotal in defining the character and feel of Independence's commercial district.

And, the major remodeling by Boatmen's Bank around 1970 has been instrumental in demonstrating the susceptibility of commercial architecture to radical alterations of their facades due to a perceived need to change appearance in order to stay competitive.

[Bank of America and Outreach International are tenants of this building as of 2013.]

Tour Stop No. 13:
Chrisman-Sawyer Bank Building [1963]
201 West Lexington Avenue

Similarly, the former Chrisman-Sawyer Bank Building located on the southwest corner has also worked to redefine the history of the Square. Originally represented by the ca. 1869 three-story, brick Italianate structure with cast iron storefront, this important corner property was first remodeled in the 1940s and then razed and replaced with the existing building in 1963.

Both corner bank buildings emphasize the significant changes that were taking place in the design of American commercial architecture during the last half of the century. Until now, the approach to new building design and remodels in existing commercial areas like the Square seldom strayed substantially from tradition. What we mean to say is that even during an up-to-date remodeling it was common for commercial structures to borrow from and blend with the design of their neighbors in size, scale, material and ornament.

But, after the mid-20th century, commercial design began to stand apart, especially in the treatment of banking institutions and office buildings. Multistory buildings erected during this period were designed to def the traditional sense of a storefront façade, and usually show little difference between the treatment of the first floor and those above. Additionally, the arrangement of window and door openings offers little indication of how interior space is arranged. In short, on Independence Square, these new buildings tend to disrupt the visual order of the streetscapes. [As of 2013, no banking services are performed in this building owned by D. Varalli Enterprises. Rather, several tenants occupy suites, including realty, law, tax and insurance companies, and a bridal shop.]

Tour Stop No. 14:
Rummell and Reick Building [1893]
104 North Liberty Avenue

Another product of early efforts in Urban Renewal is visible along this block on the west side of Independence Square. At the northwest corner of West Lexington Avenue and North Liberty Avenue, a substantial remodeling around 1965 was responsible for adding a stark façade and modern plate glass display windows to the front and side of an 1893, two-story, double-wide, brick Italianate commercial building.

Somewhat in keeping with the appearance of its remodeled neighbor to the north (most recently the Jones Store Company Building), with its wide expanse of smooth wall surface above and the original modern plate glass windows and entries below [currently (2013) boarded over since before 1999], it would appear that these alterations were an apparent attempt to keep up with the Jones' . . . and literally.

[As of 2013, the building is occupied by Gilbert, Whitney & Company, a specialty grocery and kitchenware boutique.

The store gets its name from two pioneer Latter Day Saints, Sidney Gilbert and Newel Whitney, who are associated with operating a store called, "the Lord's Storehouse," in the vacated 1827 Log Jackson County Courthouse at the southeast corner of Lexington Avenue and Lynn Streets. After nine months, on November 19, 1832, Gilbert purchased this lot and continued business for a few months; he and his family abandoned the store on November 13, 1833, fleeing a mob to safety in Clay County.

The building is named for business owners, Julius Rummell and Henry Reick, who organized a shoe store in 1888, and moved to their better and more commodious location at 104 North Liberty Avenue in 1893. Henry Reick died in 1901. In the 1906 Independence city directory, Mrs. Rosetta D. (Rummell) Reick is listed as a partnership of Mr. Rummell. Mr. Rummell died in 1925. They are all buried in Woodlawn Cemetery.[125]]

W. LEXINGTON & N. LIBERTY. LOOKING. N.W.
2-13-50

W. LEXINGTON & N. LIBERTY. LOOKING. N.W.
DEC 9 1951.

Near the completion of the remodeling of the Rummell and Reick Building in 2002, before it opened as Gilbert, Whitney & Company, a specialty grocery and kitchenware boutique.

Tour Stop No. 15:
Jones Store Company Building [early 1900s/1951]
108 North Liberty

The Jones Store Company moved to Independence Square in 1951 and substantially remodeled two, two-story, 19th-century Italianate storefronts, with a modern façade that used a curvilinear aluminum awning, mirrored plate glass windows, and a stylized department store sign.

The trend for new department store design during this period was for the building to be read as a solid mass, often a rectangle, with a simple entryway and modest graphics or fixtures attached to the wall surfaces.

This type of storefront design was a complete departure from earlier styles and, for this building, resulted in an overall effect of a massive block that dominates the streetscape and ultimately the entire West side of the Courthouse Square.

During Urban Renewal when J. C. Penney Co.
occupied the building, above; and, below, when
Jones Store Co. operated from the same location.

Tour Stop No. 16:
[ca. 1910/1990s]
110 North Liberty Avenue

Continuing the already established trend in smooth wall surfaces on this block, this ca. 1910, one-story storefront was remodeled in the late 1990s with modern stucco panels that were applied directly over the original façade. The plate glass windows on the left are also a result of this later alteration. [As of 2013, Thomson Affinity Title Company occupies this building, and part of the adjacent building.]

110 North Liberty Avenue

N. LIBERTY + W. MAPLE. LOOKING S.W.
2-13-50.

Tour Stop No. 17:
[1951]
112-114 North Liberty Avenue

The years 1950 and 1951 brought many changes to the look and feel of Independence Square. Perhaps it was in anticipation of U.S. President Harry S. Truman's homecoming from Washington, D.C., and the additional fame his legacy would bring to his hometown that the Square took on a new appearance.

The building on the southwest corner of North Liberty Avenue and West Maple Avenue, which replaced two, 19th century Victorian storefronts during a major remodeling in 1951, is an example of this new approach being taken toward commercial architecture in Independence. Much simpler and more restrained than earlier examples from the late Art Deco and Moderene periods, this façade merely hints at earlier techniques in streamlining through the use of the shiny, curvilinear awnings, decorative banding that emphasizes the horizontal, and the extensive arrangement of display windows.

[As of 2013, Thomson Affinity Title Company occupies 112 North Liberty; and, UpDog, a specialty hot dog restaurant operates from 114 North Liberty.]

Tour Stop No. 18:
Bank of Independence Building [1888/1915]
200 North Liberty Avenue

The Bank of Independence was incorporated in 1888 by five prominent Independence businessmen. This structure on the northwest corner of North Liberty Avenue and West Maple Avenue was erected the following year. [With the exception of the 1859 Jackson County Jail building (which has been known since 1959 as the 1859 Jail, Marshal's Home and Museum, one block north of the Square), this *may* be the oldest building on Independence Square.] It should also be recognized that the Bank of Independence building is the only of the three original 19th century corner bank buildings to retain its historic associations with the Courthouse Square.

Constructed in the Victorian Italianate style, the Bank of Independence building still retains much of its original character. The series of segmented arch windows with decorative limestone insets and window sills are original to the 19th century design, as is the corbelled brick cornice (or, that series of brick blocks built out from the wall, just below the roof line), and cut corner entry.

Corner Maple Ave. and Liberty St. Independence, Mo.

By 1915, when the original style of this bank building was no longer considered fashionable, a contract was let for remodeling. Newspaper accounts on October 4, 1915, described the new building as "modern in every way," with the walls on the south and east torn out and replaced by plate glass fronts and the entire interior changed, even to the fixtures. The corner entrance was retained but the original ornamental arched top doorway was removed and replaced with a much simpler limestone surround. An Italianate pressed metal pediment, originally at the roof line of the corner wall was also removed during the remodeling. Remarkably, the beautiful Victorian leaded glass transoms that were added in 1915 are still intact, just above the plate glass openings on the first floor.

The Bank of Independence operated at this site until May 6, 1961, when it moved to its new location just one-half block away on the northeast corner of North Liberty Avenue and East Truman Road (where the Jackson County Board of Election Commissioners have been headquartered since 2003).

[As of 2013, this building is vacant; most recently it had been Uptown Boutique, a women's clothing store.]

The most devastating alterations to the historic fabric of the Square took place in the early 1970s, during the a period of Urban Renewal that began around 1972 with municipal planning efforts to create an open-air pedestrian mall around the Square. This included the addition of extensive covered walkways, the evacuation of through traffic between Maple and Lexington Avenues, the construction of large plaza fountains at the east and west end of the Square, and the encapsulation of the historic courthouse lawn with massive cement walls and ramp ways.

By June 1975, the Independence cinema complex [as of 2013, Pharaoh 4 Cinemas Theater, operated by the independent Globe Cinemas Company, 114 West Maple Avenue] was developed originally as a twin-screen cinema—replacing five late-19th century and early-20th century storefronts—with a modern façade design intended to be reminiscent of the Wild West frontier town image.

A final blow by the Urban Renewal wrecking ball in 1976 was the loss of the historic Jones Hotel and Nebraska House, adjoining buildings at the northeast corner of West Maple Avenue. The Jones Hotel was first constructed in the 1840s by Lewis Jones and was considered the finest and the largest hostelry west of St. Louis. The hotel building had strong ties to the Santa Fe, Oregon and California Gold Rush Trail days and was even used as a hospital by Union Troops during the Civil War. The hotel was substantially remodeled in 1927 by T. J. Watkins, removing the last traces of the original building's exterior. However, much of the 1840 interior remained intact.

In 1976, when Urban

Renewal threatened demolition, a nomination was submitted for listing of the Jones Hotel to the National Register of Historic Places.

Unfortunately, the powers that be prevailed and that same year this valuable, historic resource was lost. The demolition of the Jones Hotel made way for the proposed construction of an uptown mall that would house variety shops, restaurants and specialty stores. Nearly 40 years later, the Jones Hotel property remains a parking lot . . . the pedestrian mall approach abandoned . . . and efforts in revitalization are focused on the importance of preserving what is left of the historic Square.

Tour Stop No. 20:
Knoepker Building [1906/1943]
106-108 West Maple Avenue

The Knoepker (pronounced "Ka-nep-ker") Store was established in 1896 by Frederick Henry Herman Knoepkner (the right side of the current building). The original 19th century, two-story, brick store burned in one of the four dramatic fires that took place on Independence Square in 1906. A new storefront was erected the same year.

In 1943, Knoepker turned over control of the business to his sons, Melvin and Carl, who, in turn, established Knoepker's Department Store. The building expanded to incorporate 108 West Maple Avenue, and the entire structure was modernized, inside and out. The importance of the Knoepker Store to the history of Independence Square is perhaps best evidenced by the fact that the building continues to display the Knoepker name.

[A selection of Knoepker family and business records are archived in the Jackson County Historical Society's Archives. As of 2013, El Pico Mexican restaurant occupies 106 West Maple, and Mockingbird Home Furnishings at 108 West Maple.]

OUR FOUNDERS

Mrs. Carrie Knoepker   Mr. Herman Knoepker

(JCHS012016BL)

Tour Stop No. 21:
Clinton Block [1906]
100-104 West Maple Avenue

The Clinton Block, as it has been called historically, also has strong ties to the Square history. Originally the home of the Smallwood Noland House, constructed around 1840 and operated as a hotel until well after the Civil War, this property was purchased by George W. Clinton before the turn-of-the-century and then remodeled for retail business use.

The Clinton Drug Store moved in on the corner, and an addition was built to the north, housing office space and a meeting room on the second floor where the City Council held its business. The Clinton Block burned February 1906, causing more than $80,000 in damage to the building and its adjoining neighbors. James Clinton, brother of George, rebuilt the Clinton corner drug store the same year. The lots to the west were sold to a new proprietor. An account taken from the *Independence Examiner*, February 21, 1906, illustrates just how important the perceived image of new commercial buildings and remodels has been throughout the history of the Square:

Tel. 191-2.

_____

. **Clinton's Drug Store** .

........is the place to get........

HEATH & MILLIGAN PAINTS,

Oils, Varnishes, Toilet
Articles and Fancy Goods.

Prescriptions a Specialty.

J. H. CLINTON.

N. E. Cor. Square.   INDEPENDENCE, MO.

_____

◄◄◄GO TO THE►►►

"The recent fires have made necessary the erection of two new business houses on the public square. The owners of the property may feel that the matter of erecting new buildings is entirely a personal one with the men who pay for them, but there is a city interest which may be excused. It is to be hoped that the new buildings will be in every way commensurate with the prominence of the location and the future development of Independence. We have too many buildings in the business part of the city of which we are not proud. A handsome new building on the pubic square is not

204

only valuable to the owner but to the town. It is an attraction to the stranger and a thing of pride and beauty to the resident."

[14-year-old Harry S. Truman enjoyed his first job in 1898 at Clinton's Drug Store when it was a true apothecary. He wrote in his memoirs:

"I was at work at 6:30 a.m. mopping floors, sweeping the sidewalk, getting everything in shipshape when Mr. Clinton came in.

"When everything was in order, there were bottles to be dusted and yards and yards of patent medicine cases and shelves to clean. I never finished the bottles and shelves before school time and had to start the next morning where I'd left off. How I hated Latin-covered prescription bottles and patent medicine shelves! "The drugstore had plate glass windows in front with a big glass jar shaped like an enlarged Greek vase in each window. Each vase was filled with colored water and oil in layers. How they kept those colors from mixing I don't know. Then the vases were surrounded by displays of patent medicine that had to be cleaned and dusted, and once a week the windows had to be washed and redecorated. "You walked through the front door onto a tile floor with showcases on each side and a soda fountain on one side in front. Behind the cases on one side were interminable rows and rows of bottles with those Latin abbreviations on them. One in particular I remember because Mr. Clinton told me to be careful not to break it. He said no more Icy

Interior of Clinton's Drug Store, around 1901.

205

Toed Feet were to be obtained. The mark on the bottle was 'Ici. Toed. Foet.' I never found out what it was.

"In the closet under the prescription case, which faced the front and shut off the view of the back end of the store, was an assortment of whiskey bottles. Early in the morning, sometimes before Mr. Clinton arrived, the good church members and Anti-Saloon Leaguers would arrive for their early morning drinks behind the prescription case at 10 cents an ounce. They would wipe their mouths, peep through the observation hole in the front of the case and depart.

"The procedure gave a 14-year old boy quite a viewpoint on the public front of leading citizens and 'amen-corner praying' churchmen.

"There were saloons aplenty around the Square in Independence and many leading men in town made no bones about going into them and buying a drink. I learned to think more highly of them than I did of the prescription counter drinkers.

"After a few months at this morning and night work, my high school studies became rather heavy, and my father suggested I quit my job and study harder, which I did."

Clinton's Drug Store later became a soda fountain when Crown Drug Store operated at this site.]

[As of 2013, Clinton's Soda Fountain operates at 100 West Maple Avenue, and Wild About Harry, a specialty gift shop "catering to men and the things they like," is located at 104 West Maple Avenue (formerly Santa Fe Furnishings Co. in 2002 when the two images at the right were taken. Apartments occupy the second floor spaces above the shops.]

Tour Stop No. 22:
Hill and Martin Hardware-Katz Drug Store Building [1906/1948]
201 North Main Street

Having sat vacant and deteriorating for nearly 20 years on the northeast corner of East Maple Avenue and North Main Street, this early 20th century brick storehouse was rehabilitated through preservation efforts in 1998, and has since operated successfully as the upscale Ophelia's Restaurant and Inn.

Most people remember this structure as the Katz Building, operated by the Katz Drug Store beginning in 1948. However, the building was actually constructed in its present form in 1906. It was built for the Hill and Martin Hardware Store after fire damaged an earlier building in one of the four dramatic fires on the Square that year. The firm later became Hill Brothers Hardware, which operated at this site until the 1948 remodeling. [Joseph and John Soldan Els operated a confectionary at this location by 1860[126] (See Meyer's 1852 engraving and the 1868 *Bird's Eye View of Independence* by Ruger for images.)]

208

The Katz Drug Store altered the original storefront by removing the entire southwest corner of the building and installing a concave wall as a background for the Katz sign. Interestingly, the materials for the original metal pylon behind the sign were manufactured by the Independence Stove Company, and was the same metallic material being used to coat the exterior of kitchen stoves. A new, angled, corner entrance and flat canopy was also added. The original center stairwell was relocated to the north end of the building and the original Victorian storefront windows were replaced with modern plate glass. All of the changes were characteristic of the later phase of the Art Deco period which was recognized by slick surfaces, rounded corners, flashy signage and a definite feeling for the role industrialization was playing in the development of commercial architecture in towns across the United States.

The 1998 rehabilitation of the Katz Building represents the first major reinvestment by a developer in a commercial building on the Square since Urban Renewal in the early 1970s.

And, while it would certainly be ideal to have preserved in perfect form the 1948 Katz Drug Store, the Jones Hotel and others lost to demolition, it is perhaps more important that we focus our attention on

the crucial role that future historic preservation efforts and continued reinvestment will play in the successful revitalization of the historic Independence Square.

209

About the
Jackson County Historical Society

The idea for the Jackson County Historical Society was first mentioned at the Independence Day celebration in 1909, when a picnic was held on the lawn of the John B. Wornall House in Kansas City, Missouri. The participants had the foresight to recognize and envision a great need for "the preservation...[and the] care and exhibition of historic articles and documents relating to Jackson County." The spirit of that 1909 gathering continues today.

Formally organized in 1940 and incorporated in 1958, the Society consists of staff, elected Board of Directors, volunteers, and a growing membership of individuals and area businesses contribute to the success of this valued not-for-profit educational organization. The Society promotes the study, appreciation, and interpretation of county history through its museum and archives, preservation and access to shared collections of historical materials, and educational programs and exhibits.

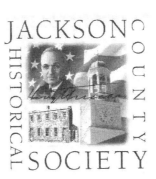

P.O. Box 4241   (816) 461-1897
Independence, MO 64051   jchs.org

Illustrations

29   1853 Courthouse Square from the northeast by A. Ruger, as pictured in the 1868 *Bird's Eye View of Independence, Missouri.* The 1859 Jail at bottom right corner has numeral "2" in the fenced, rear courtyard, JCHS004816BM.

30   George Burnett's rendition of the Second Battle of Independence, 1864. Jackson County Courthouse Square is in the distance, JCHS023518M.

31   1872 Courthouse, from the southeast, JCHS022281S.

32   1872 Courthouse, from the northeast, JCHS023832AL, courtesy James A. Tharp. A similar view (JCHS023832BL) was published in the 1877 *Illustrated Historical Atlas of Jackson County, Missouri.*)

33   Sanborn Fire Insurance Map. Independence, Missouri. August 1885.

35   1887 dedicatory plaque, JCHS025153DS, gift of David W. Jackson. The names of the County Court judges at that time, John A. McDonald, Hugh Lynch, and William C. Chiles, were inscribed in the sandstone cornerstone.

36   1887 Courthouse, from the northeast, JCHS004216BL.

37   Two views showing portions of the 1889 Annex. Left: looking from the north, JCHS0023344M. Right: Looking from the southwest corner towards Maple Avenue, JCHS001493X.

38   Removing the elevation marker so that construction in the courtyard could commence. Image courtesy Steve Noll.

39   Sanborn Fire Insurance Map. Independence, Missouri. December 1892.

40   Sanborn Fire Insurance Map. Independence, Missouri. September 1907.

41   1907 Courthouse, from the northeast, JCHS009332X.

43   Artist/architect's concept design rendering by David Frederick Wallace, 1932, JCHS006112XX.

45   Above the east and west entrances stone reliefs of an American eagle surrounded by a wreath symbolize victory and progress. Image courtesy Todd Neaves.

46   Above image courtesy Todd Neaves. Below, the Dimoush Planing Company vehicle, courtesy Carl Dimoush, JCHS025169A.

47   Massive wood beams were added to support the centralized clock tower (above). To the right: steel beams rest upon brick pillars that press firmly down onto the 1838 nucleus of the building. JCHS0251530S and JCHS025153NS, gift of David W. Jackson.

48   Jackson County Truman Courthouse clock tower belfry, with the 1879 steamboat bell at the very top of the cupola. Photo courtesy Todd Neaves.

49   Inside the clock tower remains the original clockworks, which due to the cost in maintenance, have been updated with an electronic mechanism. The ladder to the rear leads straight up to the belfry. In the recent restoration, spray foam was added between the studs for insulation. JCHS0 25153MS, gift of David W. Jackson.

50   "Results of County Planning," from the Jackson County Historical Society Archive and Research Center.

51   The Jackson County Court, 1927. Seated: Robert W. Barr; Harry S. Truman; Howard J. Vrooman. Standing: Edwin Becker, Court Deputy; Fred Boxley, County Counselor, JCHS0020391L.

52   From left to right: Thomas Bash, Judge, Western District, 1929-1930; Robert W. Barr, Judge, Eastern District, 1927-1930; Howard Vrooman, Judge, Western District, 1927-1928; Eugene I. Purcell, Judge, Eastern District, 1931-1932; Presiding Judge Harry S. Truman; W. O. Beeman, Judge, Western District, 1931-1932. Image courtesy Harry S. Truman Presidential Library and Museum, Accession No. 58-678, as found at: trumanlibrary.org.

53   Dedication Day photograph, JCHS016734L.

54   Dedication Day photograph, JCHS016735L.

55   Dedication Day photograph, JCHS016737L.

56   Dedication Day photograph, JCHS016736L.

57   Dedication Day photograph, JCHS016739L.

59   Andrew Jackson by Fred Brightman. Image courtesy David W. Jackson.

60   Thomas Jefferson by Fred Brightman. Image courtesy David W. Jackson.

62   1827 Log Jackson County Courthouse, JCHS007785L.

64   Blue Ridge Mall was the Kansas City metropolitan area's first suburban shopping mall, pictured here in the 1960s, JCHS003985L.

65   Urban renewal era on Independence Square. Gift of Steve Noll, JCHS023323BM.

67   Urban renewals' Jackson Square included a concrete courtyard; concrete walkways closing off streets; concrete fountains; and concrete covered walkways. Gift of Steve Noll, JCHS023323AM. Repeated on p. 195.

69   The Jackson County Circuit Court courtroom (today, the Brady Courtroom) as it appeared just after the 1933 remodeling when local photographer Dick Millard assisted the Jackson County Court in producing images for their book, "Results of County Planning", JCHS009499X.

70   Variation of Meyer's engraving of the 1838 Courthouse, JCHS006062XXXX.

71   Stained glass windows in the Brady Courtroom. Images courtesy David W. Jackson.

72   The jury box beyond the witness stand. Image courtesy Steve Noll.

73   Oil portrait of Hon. Joseph J. Brady, JCHS025144M, digital reproduction of the original, gift of David W. Jackson.

74   Hon. Vernon E. Scoville, III, courtesy 16th Judicial Circuit website.

75   Last Will movie poster, courtesy examiner.com.

76   Elaborate millwork and plaster were added in the Victorian era. The overhead pendant lamp is classic Art Deco from the 1933 remodeling. Image courtesy David W. Jackson.

77   Harry S. Truman around 1932, as taken by the Strauss Peyton Photographic Studio in Kansas City, Missouri, JCHS018518X.

78   Andrew Jackson equestrian statue on Independence Square, JCHS007803L.

79   Newspaper article, December 27, 1949. While the clipping is unattributed, it is either from the *Independence Examiner* or *Kansas City Star/Times.*

80-81   Items from Truman's desk, re-created in the 1970s. Images courtesy Steve Noll.

82   Jackson County Court courtroom, where Harry S. Truman presided and considered County-related matters at the beginning of the Great Depression, JCHS009498X.

83   Truman's courtroom (above) and round-shaped spectacles (below) like those that Truman wore. Images courtesy Steve Noll.

84   Original, large, payroll ledgers from the early 1930s are full of Truman's signature authenticating each person's disbursement. Image courtesy Steve Noll.

84   Judge Truman signing checks, September 24, 1927. Courtesy Harry S. Truman Presidential Library and Museum, Acc. 64-1514.

85   The courthouse courtyard as it appeared on Dedication Day, 1933. Elm trees later suffered from disease and were subsequently replaced in the 1970s, JCHS016738L.

86   Elevation showing concrete walls and steps. Image courtesy Steve Noll.

87   Dedication of an historical marker on the courthouse grounds, May 1913, JCHS001607M.

90   Jackson County Election Board employees with Bill Clinton, unknown source.

91   Worker climbs scaffolding. Image Courtesy Todd Neaves.

92   Workers inspect and replace slate roof. Images courtesy Todd Neaves.

93   On January 30, 2009, Jackson County Executive Mike Sanders announced during a news conference that the condition of Jackson County's Historic Truman Courthouse warrants officially declaring the landmark building a "public emergency." Image courtesy jacksongov.org.

94   Urban Renewal retaining walls, concrete terrace, and tons of infill soil aided to the "bathtub effect" described by Mike Sanders. Images in this chapter courtesy Steve Noll, unless otherwise noted.

95   In some locations, the retaining walls were four or five feet tall.

95   Parking on the courthouse side of the Square was lost during Urban Renewal, and restored during Phase II of the construction that began in 2009, JCHS005419L.

96   Jackson County Executive Mike Sanders at the ground-breaking.

97   Wielding sledgehammers above, left to right: Ken McClain; Jackson County Parks + Rec Director, Michele Newman; Jackson County Executive, Mike Sanders; Jackson County Public Works Director Jerry Page; and, Independence Mayor, Don Reimal. At the left: Jackson County Legislator Dennis Waits holds his golden hammer. Behind the massive walls of Urban Renewal-era concrete is the Harry S. Truman statue, shrouded for protection during the demolition project.

98   After the ground-breaking ceremony, large, heavy equipment began the process of breaking up tons of Urban Renewal-era concrete around the courthouse.

99   1933 boilers outlived their lifespan. Above shows the system prior to disassembly. Below shows the beginning of the dismantling process.

100   Each heavy piece had to be hand carried upstairs and out of the building. The remnants (above) and the foundation for a new boiler system (below).

101   The cast iron sections of the new boiler system (above) took extra large wrenches to tighten together. The completed unit (below) is smaller and much more efficient.

102   Trees and shrubs that were taken out were mulched for use as erosion control.

103   Kidwell Construction, the project contractor, took away approximately 4,000 tons of concrete and bricks from the demolition of the courthouse grounds, which were processed as backfill for road beds and other future projects.

104   Above: David W. Jackson stands beside an excavated Urban Renewal retaining wall along Lexington Avenue near Liberty, moments before its demolition (as seen at the left). Images courtesy Steve Noll and Don Potts, respectively.

105   The perimeter of the courthouse shows the natural elevation after removal of debris and re-grading.

106   New curbs and sidewalks installed resemble 1933-era infrastructure (above); Sod and historical markers were re-installed; a sprinkler system was also added to keep the lawn well-watered (below).

107   Limestone steps leading to the courthouse were carefully replaced or restored.

108   Exterior restoration of the courthouse lawn and courtyard is finished!

109   Two small spaces on each of the 1st and 2nd floor were repurposed for the elevator. Images in this chapter courtesy Steve Noll, unless otherwise noted.

110   Above: Cinderblock foundation to support the new elevator. Below: Ventilation system for heating and cooling utilizes the new boiler.

111   Outdoor and indoor views of the elevator being installed in its cinderblock shaft.

112   Archives and Research Library (2011) when previously located where Jackson County Assessment Department is today (2013). Images courtesy David W. Jackson.

113   Workmen on scaffolding surrounding the clock tower.

114   Above: Workmen busy throughout the first floor hallway. Below: Jackson County Historical Society Archive Center 2nd floor space under renovation.

115   Jackson County Historical Society Archive Center, in previously unused 2nd floor space at the southeast corner of the courthouse. Above: courtesy jacksongov.org, JCHS025153L. Below: JCHS025153L, gift of David W. Jackson.

116   The Jackson County Historical Society operates its History Center (above) and bookshop in a vault (below).

117   Across the hall, the City of Independence Tourism Department offers its Visitors' Experience Center to welcome visitors and tourists. JCHS025153PS and JCHS025153QS, gift of David W. Jackson.

118   In lower level spaces that were once dilapidated (courtesy Steve Noll), are now neat, clean, and tidy office spaces for Jackson County's Recorder of Deeds offices, JCHS025153GS, gift of David W. Jackson.

119   Jackson County's Assessment Department enjoys modern offices on the northwest corner and southwest corner (pictured above) of the main, or 1st floor level. JCHS025153HS, gift of David W. Jackson. Ample storage for the Historical Society's collections is tucked into lower level storage rooms (right, courtesy Steve Noll).

122   Unless noted, images in this chapter courtesy jacksongov.org, and incorporated into the Jackson County Historical Society photographic collections. Above: JCHS025149E. Below: JCHS025149D.

123   Above: JCHS025149C. Below: JCHS025153AS, gift of David W. Jackson.

124   Above: color guard presentation , JCHS025149A. Below: Ida McBeth performing the National Anthem, JCHS025149B.

125   Mike Sanders, Jackson County Executive, JCHS025150S.

126   Mike Sanders addresses the crow with his re-dedication speech, JCHS025149I.

127   Jackson County's Historic Truman Courthouse was re-dedicated 80 years to the day and time of its last opening in 1933, JCHS0 25149F.

129   Above: JCHS025149H. Below: JCHS025149J.

130   Above: JCHS025149K. Below: JCHS025149L.

131   Re-Dedicatory plaque installed in the south entrance of the Historic Truman Courthouse. JCHS025153CS, gift of David W. Jackson.

133   Judge Thomas Chevis, Oil on canvas, 1837, Jackson County Historical Society Collection, JCHS021290AM.

134   Bingham home in Independence, JCHS004805X. Below: "Martial Law / Order No. 11" engraving, signed by George Caleb Bingham, Jackson County Historical Society Collection, gift of Mrs. John S. Davis, JCHS021291AM.

135-136 Bingham portraits of McBride and Campbell on this and the following page provided by Patricia Moss via. Brent Schondelmeyer.

136-138 Gallery views in this chapter courtesy Steve Noll.

161   Jackson County Legislature, 2011-2014, courtesy jacksogov.org.

165   1933 Jackson County Courthouse, JCHS000188L.

166   111 North Main, JCHS004755AM.

167   100 block of North Main Street. Above: April 25, 1950, JCHS004755BM. Below: December 9, 1951, JCHS004755CM.

168   103 North Main, JCHS005554AL.

169   103 North Main, JCHS005554BL.

170 101 North Main, JCHS002014L.

172 101-103 ½ South Main Street, April 25, 1950, JCHS06013AS.

173 100 block South Main Street, October 6, 1963, JCHS006013BS.

174 100 block West Lexington Ave, April 25, 1950, JCHS005904AS.

175 100 block West Lexington Ave. Above: December 9, 1951, JCHS005904BS. Below: September 1963, JCHS005904CS.

176 105 West Lexington Avenue, JCHS025155S.

177 107 West Lexington Avenue, JCHS025156S.

178 109 West Lexington Avenue, JCHS025157S.

179 This building formerly at 111 West Lexington was destroyed by fire and was never re-built (below: JCHS025158AS). It served as a small parking lot until 2002 when it was adaptively re-used as a restaurant courtyard (above: JCHS025158BS), gifts of David W. Jackson.

180 Martin Building as it appeared around 1910. Image courtesy Harry S. Truman Presidential Library and Museum, Accession No. 62-282.

181 Martin Building [ca. 1908], 113-115 West Lexington Avenue. Above: JCHS025159S. Below: JCHS005965S.

182 Elliott Theater Building [1924], 119 West Lexington Avenue, JCHS005495AL.

183 Elliott Theater Building [1924], 119 West Lexington Avenue in 2013, by David W Jackson, JCHS005495BL.

184 Owens-Wyatt Building [ca. 1895], 121-123 West Lexington Avenue, JCHS025160AS.

185 Owens-Wyatt Building [ca. 1895], 121-123 West Lexington Avenue, JCHS025160BS,

186 First National Bank Building [originally ca. 1930; remodeled ca. 1970], 129 West Lexington Avenue January 30, 1913, JCHS001996AL.

187 First National Bank Building [originally ca. 1930; remodeled ca. 1970], 129 West Lexington Avenue April 25, 1950, JCHS001996BL.

188   Chrisman-Sawyer Bank Building [1963], 201 West Lexington Avenue in 1913, JCHS002885AL.

189   Above: Chrisman-Sawyer Bank Building [1963], 201 West Lexington Avenue, April 25, 1950, JCHS002885BL. Below: ca. 1960s, JCHS002885CL.

190   Rummell and Reick Building [1893], 104 North Liberty Avenue, JCHS001498L, Gary Plowman-Studio Three Collection of P. H. Grinter Photographs.

191   Rummell and Reick Building [1893], 104 North Liberty Avenue, September, 1963, JCHS006015CS.

192   Rummell and Reick Building [1893], 104 North Liberty Avenue. Above: February 13, 1950, JCHS006015AS. Below: December 9, 1951, JCHS006015BS.

193   Near the completion of the remodeling of the Rummell and Reick Building in 2002, before it opened as Gilbert, Whitney & Company, a specialty grocery and kitchenware boutique. Images courtesy David W. Jackson.

195   Above: Urban renewals' Jackson Square included a concrete courtyard; concrete walkways closing off streets; concrete fountains; and concrete covered walkways. Gift of Steve Noll, JCHS023323AM (repeated on page 67). Below: Jones Store Company Building [early 1900s/1951], 108 North Liberty, prior to Urban Renewal, JCHS025161S.

196   100 block of North Liberty Avenue, February 13, 1950, JCHS025162AS.

197   100 block of North Liberty Avenue, December 9, 1951, JCHS025162BS.

198   Bank of Independence Building [1888/1915], 200 North Liberty Avenue, JCHS000157PC.

199   Bank of Independence Building [1888/1915], 200 North Liberty Avenue, JCHS025163S.

200   North side of Square, 100 Block West Maple Avenue, JCHS006014S.

201   North side of Square, 100 Block West Maple Avenue. Above: April 25, 1950, JCHS025164A. Below: December 9, 1951, JCHS025164B.

202   Knoepker's co-founders, JCHS012016BL, gift of the Richard Harrison family.

203   Above: Knoepker Building [1906/1943], 106-108 West Maple Avenue, JCHS011997S, by Richard Harrison. Below: North side of Square, 100 Block West Maple Avenue, JCHS006012S.

204   Clinton's Drug Store advertisement, courtesy Harry S. Truman Library website.

205   Interior of Clinton's Drug Store, around 1901. Courtesy Harry S. Truman Presidential Library, Accession No. 63-14.

206   J. H. Clinton's Pharmacy advertisement, courtesy Harry S. Truman Library website.

207   Above: Clinton building, looking north on Main Street, JCHS005905S. Middle: Clinton's and Ophelia's, looking northeast at Maple Avenue and Main Streets. Below: Clinton Block [1906], 100-104 West Maple Avenue, 2002, courtesy David W. Jackson.

208   Hill and Martin Hardware-Katz Drug Store Building [1906/1948], 201 North Main Street. Maple and Main, looking northeast (not Liberty, as identified on the image), May 19, 1950. This popular image is available through the Harry S. Truman Library; a copy is available as JCHS023170AL.

209   Hill and Martin Hardware-Katz Drug Store Building [1906/1948], 201 North Main Street. Maple and Main, looking northeast. Above: JCHS023170BL. Below: Ophelia's, 2002, courtesy David W. Jackson.

Notes

[1] Taylor, Jon E. "Significance of the Jackson County Courthouse and Square on the Life of Harry S. Truman." Jackson County (Mo.) Historical Society Archives, Historic Truman Courthouse Restoration Records, Friends of the Courthouse Files, Document ID 276.02F3.

[2] For consistency, the courthouse dates that follow pertain to the first year of occupation.

[3] Missouri General Assembly Session Laws (aka. Laws of Missouri), Volume II, published in 1842, pages 83-84. When a new county was organized by the Missouri General Assembly, the legislative act appointed commissioners who were to select a county seat.

[4] Burke, Charles. "Some residents have called 1827 Log Courthouse home," *Independence* (Mo.) *Examiner*, 23 Mar. 1987. Lewis was grandson of Hannah Boone, Daniel Boone's sister, according to Bess L. Hawthorne in, "Hannah Boone and Her Descendants," courtesy Gayle Gresham via. e-mail [gcgresham@msn.com] to David W. Jackson, June 2013, where she further stated Daniel P. Lewis' daughter, Elizabeth, married Wilburn Christison; he was born in Jackson County in 1827. The Christisons, Gresham's great great grandparents lived in Platte County in the 1850s and joined the ranks with other Missourians who crossed the River to vote in the Kansas elections. Wilburn was a delegate to the Lecompton Constitutional Convention, after he had moved to Kansas. His father was Adam Christison, who lived in Jackson County in 1880, but died soon after.

[5] Burke, 23 Mar. 1987.

[6] James Shepherd had three slaves in 1820 when he and his family lived in Lee County, Virginia.[6] At that time, his slave, Samuel, was about 10-years-old, give or take a year. The Shepherds emigrated to Jackson County in 1824. The 1830 U.S. Census for Jackson County revealed that Shepherd had seven slaves. By 1840, there were eight slaves; Samuel would have been about 30-years-old. Samuel had a brother named Peter; however, no other mention or data has been located about Peter Shepherd. After James Shepherd died in 1846, according to Jackson County probate records, his slaves were sold for the purpose of dividing the estate among his heirs. Samuel was sold to Major Edwin A. Hickman, a farmer who operated a combined grist and saw mill where Fairmount Park was later located on West 24 Highway, Independence, Missouri. In 1850, Hickman owned three slaves: a 33-year-old male (Samuel was actually more like 40; slaves' ages were almost always approximated, as birth records were rarely, if ever, maintained); a 24-year-old male; a 24-year-old female; and 3-year-old female. During the

Civil War, Samuel fled to Lawrence, Kansas. His first appearance as a freedman is in the 1865 Kansas State Census. Henceforth, his name was always spelled "Samuel Shepard." Samuel was enumerated as a 55-year-old farmer (this was the most accurate recording of his age) along with his wife, Julia A. (Newson) Shepard, a Kentucky native, and two children: John Shepard, born around 1849, and Martha Shepard, born around 1851. The family also appears in the 1870 U.S. Census in the same location, when Samuel reported being 60-years-old (again, the most accurate recording of his age). When the 1875 Kansas State Census was taken, Samuel--who said he was then 75 [actually 65]--was living with his daughter, Martha "Mattie," then wife of Joshua Hamilton. Samuel still lived with them a quarter-century later in 1900, when he *claimed* to have been born in April 1790, and was 110-years-old [actually 90]. This is the first and only instance where a middle initial of "D" was ever provided. While April is likely his accurate birth month, something celebrated annually, his actual birth year had become quite inflated.
Samuel lived and died in Lawrence, Kansas, and his advanced age became the stuff of legend. At the time of his death in 1909, he was reportedly 125-years-old [actually 99], and his relatives erected a tombstone with his birth having occurred in 1784. The 1865 and 1870 census returns appear to be the most consistent and believable recordings of Samuel's actual age, which would place his birth date around 1810. Therefore, it would be more reliable to state that Samuel Shepard was 99-years-old when he died. Still, nothing short of a miracle; and just imagine all the Shepard descendants. There were a number of years after the 1870 Census when Samuel and Julia were no longer enumerated together. She appears separately in several census enumerations through 1910. Still, Samuel and Julia are buried side-by-side in the Oak Hill Cemetery, Lawrence, Kansas, where their descendants erected a marker over their graves. Historical research for this biographical vignette was provided by local historian, James A. Tharp, and is filed in Jackson County (Mo.) Historical Society Archives Document ID Vertical File Newspaper Subject Files: Biography: Shepherd. See also Hickman, W. Z. *History of Jackson County, Missouri*. Reprinted 1990 by Southern Historical Press, Inc. (Topeka, Ks.: Historical Publishing Company, 1920), 235-237. Stillwell, Ted. W. "Sam Shepard and the broadaxe," *Independence* (Mo.) *Examiner*, 16 Sept. 1998; and, Garrison, Alex. "Legend of 125-year-old stirs curiosity in Lawrence," Lawrence Journal-World, 29 June 2012.

[7] "Before Kansas City Existed," *Kansas City* (Mo.) *Star*, 29 July 1905. Abner E. Adair was born in Independence in 1832. The father of Abner E. Adair bought the first lot ever sold in Independence in 1827. He brought the first thoroughbred stallion to Jackson County when he came to Missouri Territory from Kentucky in 1818. Abner E. Adair, with F. X. Aubrey and a party of 18 men were the first European-Americans to explore what became the Arizona Territory. His brother, Joseph Adair, was the first Caucasian child born in Independence. Both brothers relocated in later life to Clinton, Missouri.

[8] County Court minutes, Volume 1, page 136, as discovered and published by Pauline Siegfried Fowler, "1831 Unchronicled Courthouse," *Jackson County Historical Society JOURNAL* (September 1973), p. 6-7, 9.

[9] *Jackson* (Independence, Mo.) *Examiner*, 31 January, 1919, cover, c.1; 9 Jan. 1920, p. 4, c. 5; 14 May 1920, p. 4. c. 5; 23 July 1920, p. 5, c.1; 10 Dec. 1920, p. 4, c. 1; 26 May 1922, p. 4, c. 4. *Independence* (Mo.) *Examiner*, 29 Apr. 1920, cover; 18 June 1920, p. 3; 16 Nov. 1921, p.3.

[10] *Independence* (Mo.) *Examiner*, 1 June 1972.

[11] Gentry, Sue. "Journalism Group Meets Tonight in County's First Courthouse," *Independence* (Mo.) *Examiner*, 16 Sept. 1952. Also, "Jackson county's First Courthouse is Example as 'Good Restoration,'" *Independence* (Mo.) *Examiner*, 26 Feb. 1962.

[12] Letter from Jerry Winkelman to Kathleen Tuohey, 6 Dec. 1994, recalling a story told to him about 1963 by Jess James, retired Independence Police officer; Jackson County (Mo.) Historical Society Archives, Document ID 242F7. It was, however, a common occurrence for slaves to be auctioned as a matter of probate to settle an estate. Oftentimes, those transactions were recorded in the County Court minutes. While Liberty, Clay County, Missouri, also held an annual slave auction each January on their courthouse steps, it is not known at this publication's date if such an event transpired in Jackson County.

[13] Steele, Patrick H., Jr. "Wind the Clock: A Guided Tour of Architecture on the Historic Independence Square, National Historic Preservation Week, May 8-15, 1999." Jackson County (Mo.) Historical Society Archives Document ID 84F32.

[14] *Kansas City* (Mo.) *Star*, and 30 July 1905 and 7 Aug. 1932.

[15] County Court minutes, Volume 1, page 52, as located and published by Pauline Siegfried Fowler, "1831 Unchronicled Courthouse," *Jackson County Historical Society JOURNAL* (September 1973), p. 6-7, 9.

[16] County Court minutes, Volume 1, page 70, as located and published by Pauline Siegfried Fowler, "1831 Unchronicled Courthouse," *Jackson County Historical Society JOURNAL* (September 1973), p. 6-7, 9.

[17] County Court minutes, Volume 1, page 71, as located and published by Pauline Siegfried Fowler, "1831 Unchronicled Courthouse," *Jackson County Historical Society JOURNAL* (September 1973), p. 6-7, 9.

[18] County Court minutes, Volume 1, page 36, 71, 93, as located and published by Pauline Siegfried Fowler, "1831 Unchronicled Courthouse," *Jackson County Historical Society JOURNAL* (September 1973), p. 6-7, 9. At the November 1827 session the County Court authorized the superintendent to alter the specifications if necessary, and if such changes would reduce expenses to the County. The finishing of only two fireplace hearths indicates one change which was made under this discretionary order, for the plans called for two fireplaces on each of the two floors in the east end, and two fireplaces only on the first floor in the west end. That other alterations were made was indicated when Boggs reported on August 3, 1829, that the contract for the brick and stone work was satisfactorily completed, including, "...such alterations in the original plans," which he, Boggs, had been authorized to make.

[19] County Court minutes, Volume 1, page 113, as located and published by Pauline Siegfried Fowler, "1831 Unchronicled Courthouse," *Jackson County Historical Society JOURNAL* (September 1973), p. 6-7, 9.

[20] Fowler writes, "It brought the court nothing but headaches. The fireplaces did not provide enough heat; room rent had to be paid now and then for the clerk to use other quarters; building repairs were almost constantly needed; and the second floor had a great hole in it. The hole, which was 15-feet wide and 20-feet long, was designed to be finished as an attractive gallery to receive the staircase to the second floor. But, in point of fact the entire second floor must have been impractical to heat in the Missouri winters. Finally, on August 17, 1836, the court allowed the citizens of Independence to close this hole (I suppose by building a trap door) by removing the plank with which the ceiling of the Grand Jury room had been covered so that they might hold meetings in the second story for their Thespian Society." County Court minutes, Volume 2, page 200.

[21] Jackson County Court minutes, Volume 2, p. 232, as located and published by Pauline Siegfried Fowler, "1831 Unchronicled Courthouse," *Jackson County Historical Society JOURNAL* (September 1973), p. 6-7, 9. Mrs. Fowler mentions Volume 2 having been missing for 15 years (by 1970), which means it had not been located since about 1955. Later in the article she says that Milton Perry "found and handed me the missing volume," on August 15, 1971. She does not indicate if that was the original, handwritten volume, or the typewritten copy from the 1930s. At the conclusion of her article, however, she says in reference to previous researchers negating the 1831 courthouse, "Perhaps they found the original script too difficult to decipher," and notes "For instance, W. Z. Hickman, History of Jackson County, Mo., 1920, 142, quoted the record as "…including the present temporary courthouse and lot 1…" when in fact the "1" is a large, heavy comma. The log courthouse was located on lot 59 until moved to its present location."

[22] Historically, attributed as 1836.

[23] Jackson County Court minutes, 19 Dec. 1836, Volume 2, p. 232.

[24] Jackson County Court minutes, 6 Feb. 1837, Volume 2, p. 245. On 7 Feb. 1838 (Volume 2, p. 361), the Court appointed Thomas H. Wilson as Superintendant to replace "Henry Chiles, deceased."

[25] Jackson County Court minutes, 20 Feb. 1837, Volume 2, p. 269.

[26] "Daniel King undertook the building of the brick and stone work on the new Courthouse" for $3,500 (20 Feb. 1837, Volume 2, p. 269). He was partially paid on 22 Aug. 1837 (Volume 2, p. 304); and another "10 percent on the amount due," on 10 May 1838 (Volume 2, p. 401). John Parker was allowed a similar payment on 20 Sept. 1838 (Volume 3, p. 27) for "the [carpentry] work done on the Courthouse." It is, therefore, the opinion of this author, David W. Jackson, that the completion date of the, "first, permanent, brick Courthouse on Independence Square was most likely September 1838, not 1836. Noting some factual inaccuracies, see also, "Citizens Helped to Rebuild County Courthouse in 1837," *Independence* (Mo.) *Examiner*, 27 Aug. 1937.

[27] Jackson County Court minutes, Volume 3, p. 182, as located and published by Pauline Siegfried Fowler, "1831 Unchronicled Courthouse," *Jackson County Historical Society JOURNAL* (September 1973), p. 6-7, 9.

[28] Jackson County Court Minutes, 4 May 1841, Volume 3, p. 383; and, 3 Feb. 1842, Volume 3, p. 532.

[29] Jackson County Court Minutes, July 1844 (p. 19) and August 1844 (p. 63), courtesy Nancy M. Ehrlich, who also noted on August 7 (p. 63) two separate entries for the sale of slaves at auction "at the Courthouse door," from the Jesse Overton and William Moore estates.

[30] "Missouri Heritage," *Kansas City* (Mo.) *Star*, 16 Dec. 1967.

[31] Meyer, Hermann. Meyer's Universe, or, Views and Descriptions of the Most Interesting and Remarkable Places and Objects, Both Natural and Manmade, In the Entire World. Volume 19. (Hildburghausen and New York: Bibliographic Institute, 1857), 73-74. This complete German to English translation of the "Independence Courthouse" section is provided courtesy James A. Tharp. It is interesting to note that Meyer's engraving "taken from nature" in 1852 was not published until 1857 . . . AFTER the Courthouse had already undergone its 1853 renovation.

[32] "County Solved Flea Problem at Courthouse," *Independence* (Mo.) *Examiner*, 26 Feb. 1962; previously published in the *Examiner, 27 Jul 1905*, when the story was authenticated and vouched for by a "well known authority on such matters, Uncle Jim Peacock," who was police court judge at that time. Another *Examiner* article from 27 Aug. 1937, records "The late Judge James Peacock used to relate an amusing story about how the courthouse, during its occupancy by soldiers, became infested with fleas.

[33] Jackson, David W. and Paul Kirkman. *LOCK DOWN: Outlaws, Lawmen and Frontier Justice in Jackson County, Missouri.* (Independence, Mo.: Jackson County Historical Society, 2009), 21.

[34] McDermott, John Francis. *Travels in Search of the Elephant: The Wanderings of Alfred S. Waugh, Artist, in Louisiana, Missouri, and Santa Fe, in 1845-1846.* (St. Louis, Mo.: Missouri Historical Society, 1951), 40. Wood Noland was Smallwood Veatch Noland. Waugh painted a portrait of General Samuel D. Lucas, who was for many years the clerk for both the Jackson County Court and Jackson County Circuit Court.

[35] McDermott, 41-43. Lucas had played a leading part in the "Mormon Wars" of the 1830s in western Missouri and had risen to the rank of major-general commanding the Fourth Division of the Missouri Militia.

[36] Jackson, David W. *Direct Your Letters to San Jose: The California Gold Rush Letters and Diary of James and David Lee Campbell.* (Kansas City, Mo.: The Orderly Pack Rat, 2000). 65,000 is a defensible figure according to http://www.octa-trails.org/learn/trail_facts.php (viewed 3 Apr 2013). Also, http://en.wikipedia.org/wiki/Oregon_Trail (viewed 1 April 2013).

[37] Historically, this rendition of the building has been attributed as 1848; but, historical records place the date at 1853.

[38] County Court Minutes, Volume 9, page 383, 28 Jul 1852, involve a petition to build an addition to the Courthouse. The Courthouse is also mentioned in Volume 11, page 128.

[39] Ohman, Marian M. Missouri Courthouses: Jackson County. Department of Community Development, University of Missouri-Columbia. (http://muextension.missouri.edu/xplor/uedivis/ue6047.htm viewed 23 May 2001).

[40] Recollection relayed to the author by Nancy M. Ehrlich, who shared this story that Rufus Burrus II had told her some years before.

[41] "Rich and Honored: Jackson County Career of William McCoy of Independence," *Kansas City* (Mo.) *Journal*, 3 July 1899, as located and shared with the author bySharon Snyder and Nancy M. Ehrlich.

[42] "Citizens Helped to Rebuild…"

[43] Jackson County Court Minutes, July, 1863, 12:100600. In January 1863, J. W. Harvey was paid $5 to remove the Courthouse courtyard fence (12:100472). On March 2, 1863, the roof was repaired in preparation for the Circuit Court session (12:100510), with thanks to Nancy M. Ehrlich, who also found Yager (1860 U.S. Census spelling) was a master carpenter; Burford was director of Independence Branch of the Southern Bank of St. Louis; and, Carpenter was a Rhode Island-born farmer living south of 24 near Salem Church. Ehrlich also found the notation that, "most of the wounded have been taken to Kansas. Those that were not able to be moved, are at the courthouse, are well taken care of, and are getting along well. There are nineteen or twenty here," in the *Cleveland Morning Leader* (Cleveland, Ohio), 3 Sept. 1862, (http://chroniclingamerica.loc.gov.lccn/sn83035142/1862-09-03/ed-1/seq-1/ viewed 3 Apr. 2013).

[44] Jackson County Court Minutes, in April 1864 the Sheriff was ordered to have the Courthouse dome and roof repaired (12:100759). He sold tin off the Courthouse for $1 (12:100765), and had the cupola and dome painted (12:100770). Nancy M. Ehrlich added that on April 4, 1864, the County Court paid J. C. Atkins $70.90 to replace glass (Jackson County Court Minutes (12:101771); and, on May 2, 1864, paid Pollard and Fairman $470 for repairing the Courthouse roof (12:100794 and 12:100800).

[45] Jackson County Court Minutes, provided by Nancy M. Ehrlich, Vol. 12, p. 336. Other Jackson County Court Minutes located by the author include a July 7, 1865, entry where the Sheriff was ordered to have roof of Courthouse and cupola repaired to prevent leaking; have the lightening rod mended; banisters to stairs repaired; the door repaired; and, locks put on those needed; and have the east door of the Courthouse repaired (or replaced) (12:101203); a May1866, entry ordering repair the Courthouse and building a plank fence around the courtyard (13:101809); a July 1866 entry, paying John D. Warren $3,000 for repairing Courthouse and courtyard fence (13:101952); and, a June 1867 entry paying George C. Bryant $112 for work on the Courthouse fence (14:103079).

[46] Old War Claims Paid," *The Blue & Grey Chronicle*. (June 2013): 16: 5: 12-13.

[47] Birdsall, 490. "Major A. B. Cross Dead," *Kansas City* (Mo.) *Star*, 18 Aug. 1894, 1.

[48] Kansas City (Mo.) Star, 7 Aug. 1932.

[49] [Independence] *Centennial Greetings, 1827-1927: Wishing Our City Prosperity in its Second Century*, by the Lambert Moon Printing Company. Jackson County (Mo.) Historical Society Archives Document ID 76F28.

[50] The Sentinel (Independence, Mo.), 9 Jun 1877.

[51] Missouri General Assembly Session Laws (aka. Missouri Statutes), 1887.

[52] Gentry, Sue. "Remodeling let courthouse grow to fit county," *Independence* (Mo.) *Examiner*, 29 Jan. 1987.

[53] "Independence Courthouse is Studded with Memorials," *Independence* (Mo.) *Examiner*, 29 Oct. 1937.

[54] Gentry, Sue. "Courthouse Clock: In Use Since 1879," *Independence* (Mo.) *Examiner*, 7 Oct. 1963; and "It's Striking Again! Old Town Clock is Tolling the Hours," *Independence* (Mo.) *Examiner*, 22 Apr. 1972. The 1879 date has not been substantiated elsewhere, and 'may' refer to the date of the riverboat bell used to toll the hour. Also, Fox, Jeff. "Courthouse Bell Will Chime Again," *The* (Independence, Mo.) *Examiner*, 13 July 2013.

[55] "Courthouse, " *Jackson* (Independence, Mo.) *Examiner*, 4 Mar. 1904. Jesse Martin, in charge of the tin shop at Mize Hardware climbed the iron framework of the spire and took down the broken arrow and made a new one. He also made a gilded ball 14-inches in circumference which he placed on the rod above the arrow. The big arrow, 7-feet-long, was set in place after 'false scaffolding' was built so the workmen could reach the top.

[56] Ohman states that the next major alteration began in 1905 when a new division of the Circuit Court was established in Independence.

[57] County Court minutes, March 1906, as presented by Ohman.

[58] *Independence* (Mo.) *Examiner*, 6 and 9 June and 13 Oct. 1906.

[59] In May 1906, the County Court contracted with Chris Yetter, as per Ohman.

[60] Zimmer, Ruth. "Courthouse bell may toll…if there is one," *Independence (Mo.) Examiner*, 30 Dec. 1975. Also, "But it doesn't ring: Courthouse Bell Really There," *Independence (Mo.) Examiner*, 31 Dec. 1975.

[61] Snyder, Brian K. "Harry Truman's Courthouse and Beyond." Three-leave manuscript, possibly draft text for a subsequently published article. Jackson County (Mo.) Historical Society Archives, Document ID 276.01-276.03. Snyder continues, "Judge Harry Truman's public improvement project was a huge success and was touted in a 122-page book entitled *Results of County Planning, Jackson County, Missouri*. Harry Truman took these successes with him to Washington D.C. In the summer of 1947 while at a speaking engagement at the University of Virginia, surrounded by the architecture of Thomas Jefferson, President Truman was inspired to add a balcony to the south portico of the White House. He even imagined that he would be fulfilling a plan that Jefferson himself would have implemented. Months later, President Truman would begin to notice signs of deterioration of the White House structure itself. One of the grand chandeliers swayed from just foot traffic while its support chain had stretched to its limits and was near failure. One of Margaret Truman's pianos actually broke through the floor. [A special] commission would eventually recommend the historic preservation alternative and the nation was about to implement one of its largest restoration project in its history. The exterior walls were to remain and be restored. The interior structure would be dismantled and reconstructed with the addition of a two-story basement. The entire structure would be supported and reinforced with modern materials combined with updates for security and modern conveniences for a total cost of $5,761,000." Details of the bond figures are described on pages 9 and 121 of *Results of County Planning*.

[62] Recollection relayed to the author by Nancy M. Ehrlich, who shared this story that had been told to her some years before by either Jim Ryan, Patrick O'Brien, or Bill Curtis.

[63] Correspondence between Carl Dimoush and David W. Jackson, February 2004 and June 2013, on file in the Jackson County Historical Society Administrative Records, Archives Research Correspondence Files, David W. Jackson, Director, 2000-2013.

[64] Fox, Jeff. "Courthouse Bell Will Chime Again," *The* (Independence, Mo.) *Examiner*, 13 July 2013.

[65] Boardman, Maxine (Moore), recollection, "Civil War Sword 'Points' to one of History's Mysteries, Jackson County (Mo.) Historical Society Archives, Document ID 70F22. Debs ran as the Socialist Party's candidate for the presidency in 1900, 1904,. 1908, 1912, and 1920, the last time from a prison cell.

[66] Independence resident and amateur artist, Fred F. Brightman, donated these two categorical paintings for the newly renovated Jackson County Courthouse in September 1933. Brightman, son of Samual C. and Jenecta (Forhee) Brightman, was born in Green Top, Schuyler County, Missouri, on July 28, 1866. There he taught school in his young adulthood. He moved to Independence in 1895. In 1908, was editor of the *Independence Daily Democrat*. In that year, he was allegedly accosted with a knife by William N. Southern, editor of the *Independence Sentinel*. He later became the Independence correspondent for the *Kansas City Journal Post* newspaper for about 20 years until he retired in 1931. On July 7, 1917, Brightman was married Elizabeth Moore. Brightman 67 when the paintings were donated in 1933. Nothing is known about his artistic interests, background or education. Nor are there any other known paintings by him to survive in public view. The couple lived in the mansion at 126 South Pleasant Street, and furnished it with antiques which had been collected through the years and many years. They sold the mansion and moved to 109 South Pendleton in 1937. He often said that he was not a collector but just "saved interesting things." Unfortunately three house fires destroyed quite a few items in that home. Brightman was a charter member of the Independence Browning Society, organized in 1926. He played the title role in the Pied Piper which the Society presented annually for several years. Brightman died at the Independence Sanitarium on 8 Dec. 1950, and is buried beside his wife in Mound Grove Cemetery, Independence, Missouri. He was survived by a sister, Miss Bessie Brightman, and a brother, George Brightman, of Lancaster, Missouri. See *Kansas City* (Mo.) *Star*, 2 Dec. 1908; Brightman's marriage and death certificates, and obituary in the *Independence* (Mo.) *Examiner*, 9 Dec. 1950.

[67] *Independence (Mo.) Examiner*, 5 Sept. 1932.

[68] While the Courthouse was being remodeled between 1932 and 1933, the Jackson County Court ordered on October 31, 1932, that County offices were to be relocated, as follows:

Circuit Court:	Independence City Hall
Probate Court:	Telephone Building, 308 W Maple Ave
Treasurer:	210 W Maple Ave
Recorder:	Jackson County Bank Building, 205 W Lexington Ave
Surveyor & Highway Engineer:	2nd floor, Martin Building, 113-115 W Lexington Ave
Clerk of the Circuit	

Court & Sheriff:	2nd floor, Masonic Building, nw corner Kansas and Main
Collector & Assessor:	1st floor, Masonic Building
Clerk and Office of County Court:	Home Deposit Trust Building, 125 W Lexington Ave **(This is where Presiding Judge Harry S. Truman's temporary office was located during the remodeling.)**
County Court:	1827 Log Jackson County Courthouse, 117 W Kansas Ave **(This is where the County Court held legislative sessions.)**

This data compiled courtesy Randy Diehl, Jackson County Public Works, as located in the Jackson County Court minutes.

[69] For many years between the 1950s and 2013, it was called the Jackson County Courthouse Annex. "Time, Wear Take Toll at Two Courthouses," Kansas City (Mo.) Times, 25 May 1967. Also, a small collection of undated clippings in the Jackson County (Mo.) Historical Society Archives Vertical File Clipping Collection—Biography: Brady.

[70] http://deadmalls.com/malls/blue_ridge_mall.html (viewed 1 April 2013).

[71] http://capd.ksu.edu/media/pdfs/kcdc-streetcars-by-kyle-sherwood.pdf (viewed 1 April 2013).

[72] Taylor, Jon E. A President, a Church, and Trails West: Competing Histories in Independence, Missouri. (Columbia, University of Missouri Press, 2008), 101.

[73] *Independence (Mo.) Examiner*, 17 July 1967. A capital improvements bond issue required the County Court to take *some* action with the old courthouse.

[74] Comprehensive Development Plan for Independence, Missouri. http://www.ci.independence.mo.us/userdocs/comdev/Chapter%201%20Background.pdf (viewed 18 July 2013).

[75] Similarly, the northeast corner of the 1838 Courthouse may also be seen in the City of Independence's Visitor Experience Center .

[76] Recollection provided courtesy of local historian, Nancy M. Ehrlich.

[77] "Judge Reminisces as he readies for Court move," *Independence (Mo.) Examiner*, 8 June 1972, 8B.

[78] *Independence* (Mo.) *Examiner*, 8 June 1972, 8B. Brady was born and raised in Independence. His father, Charles W. Brady, was a well-known grocer and twice a postmaster. Judge Brady graduated from the Kansas City School of Law in 1933 and received his juris doctor degree from the University of Missouri. He conducted a private practice of law for a number of years. He was elected Independence justice of the peace in 1943, and served until he was elected to the bench of the Sixth District. Brady had county-wide jurisdiction, but magistrates usually handle only cases in the district in which they were elected. For many years, Judge Brady's district covered all areas in Jackson County outside Kansas City. Later the Seventh District was created in the south part of the County. The magistrate used to handle parole matters, but that was taken over by the state parole board. The case load increased when magistrates were given the jurisdiction to handle civil cases involving damages up to $3,500. The previous limit had been $1,500. The court also handled criminal cases; but, with limited power. In felony

cases, the magistrates have the power to dismiss, but if there is sufficient evidence for a trial, the cases are bound over to the Circuit Court.

[79] "Building Jackson County," Whistle Stop: Harry S. Truman Library Institute Newsletter (1985): 13:2:2.

[80] One local resident told the author that some miscreants on the night before the statue unveiling had placed a large pile of manure on the ground underneath the horse's hind end. The author thought this tid-bit too creative a stunt to let it be forgotten.

[81] "President Back in Familiar Spot at Courthouse," *Independence* (Mo.) *Examiner*, 27 Dec. 1949.

[82] The IBM 'master' clock ran 'slave' clocks through electronic impulses. The 'slave' in the Truman Courtroom was produced by Hahl Automatic Clock Co. Hahl produced clocks in 1933; but, they started much earlier than IBM, and their 'slaves were run by a sophisticated *pneumatic process*. Without further investigation, it appears that the two defunct clocks that survive may not have direct relationship to one another.

[83] Fowler, Larry. "Courtroom Remodeling in Style of Truman Era," Kansas City (Mo.) Star, 11 May 1972.

[84] Gentry, Sue. "Local Gentry: Old Courtroom Yarns Recalled," *Independence* (Mo.) *Examiner*, undated clipping in the Jackson County Historical Society Vertical Clipping Subject Files: Jackson County Courthouses. It is estimated to be June 1973 judging from data on the reverse of the clipping.

[85] Davis, Mike. "Truman Courtroom to be restored," Jackson County (Blue Springs, Mo.) Sentinel, 16 Mar. 1972. Also, Burke, Charles. "Courtroom Takes on 20's Era Flavor," *Independence* (Mo.) *Examiner*, 3 Aug. 1973.

[86] "County Court Nostalgia Recalled in Old Independence Courthouse," *Independence* (Mo.) *Examiner*, 30 Mar 1972.

[87] http://www.examiner.net/jackie/x931215503/Cindy-McClain-Perpetual-motion-on-the-Square?zc_p=1 (viewed 3 Apr 2013).

[88] Lamb, Amy. "Facelift in our future," *Independence* (Mo.) *Examiner*, 21 Apr. 1995.

[89] Dornbrook, James. "Jan. 30 finish slated," *Independence* (Mo.) *Examiner*, 31 Oct. 2002.

[90] "Saving the Jackson County Truman Courthouse," http://www.jacksongov.org/content/3624/default.aspx (viewed 3 March 2013).

[91] This section obtained primarily from, "Saving the Jackson County Truman Courthouse," and press releases posted and cross-linked at: http://www.jacksongov.org/content/3624/default.aspx (viewed 3 March 2013).

[92] Mike Sanders Re-Dedication speech, Jackson County's Historic Truman Courthouse Restoration Records, Jackson County (Mo.) Historical Society Archives, Document ID 276.02F20.

[93] Jackson County Court minutes, 12:160:100246.

[94] Ibid., 12:160:100246.

[95] Ibid., 12:176:100326; and, 12:205:100483.

[96] Ibid., 12:190; and, 12:300:100830.

[97] Ibid., 12:180:100346.

[98] Ibid., 12:225:100570.

[99] Ibid., 12:305:100856.

[100] Ibid., 12:241:100653.

[101] Ibid., 12:355:101115.

[102] Ibid., 13:432:101833.

[103] Jackson, David W. "Jackson County's Poor Farm Transformed into a Rich Healthcare Center." *Jackson County Historical Society JOURNAL* (Spring 2004):45: 1: 8-13. The name changed to "The Jackson County Home for the Aged," and later, "Jackson County Home for the Aged and Infirm." African-Americans were segregated in the mid- to late-1920s to separate facilities across Lee's Summit Road to the east.

[104] Truman's loss to Rummell was the only election where Truman was ever defeated.

[105] Appointed March 31, 1975.

[106] Appointed December 8, 1980.

[107] Appointed November 2, 1981.

[108] Appointed May 11, 1981.

[109] Appointed March 19, 1979.

[110] Appointed April 18, 1983.

[111] Appointed December 2, 1985.

[112] Appointed February 11, 1985.

[113] Appointed July 1, 1985.

[114] Appointed May 15, 1989.

[115] Appointed May 30, 1989.

[116] Appointed January 25, 1993.

[117] Appointed April 25, 1994.

[118] Appointed October 14, 1996.

[119] Appointed January 12, 2000.

[120] Appointed April 1, 2003.

[121] Appointed January 18, 2005.

[122] Jackson County (Mo.) Historical Society Archives, Document ID 84F32.

[123] Soldan Els genealogy, Jackson County (Mo.) Historical Society Archives, Document ID 256F15.

[124] Soldan Els genealogy, Jackson County (Mo.) Historical Society Archives, Document ID 256F15.

[125] Anderson, Terry L. *Come and Spit on the Floor and Make Yourself at Home: A History of Independence and Jackson County from the News Stories of the Jackson Examiner, 1898-1900.* Volume 1. (Independence, Mo.: Terry L. Anderson, 1995), 38-39. Also, Missouri Death Certificates and Woodlawn Cemetery tombstone inscription indices.

[126] Soldan Els genealogy, Jackson County (Mo.) Historical Society Archives, Document ID 256F15.

Index

239

240

241

242

Made in the USA
Columbia, SC
13 May 2017